A VISITOR'S GUIDE TO THE
FALKLAND ISLANDS

The essential Guide for visitor: ng the ations in the Islands

First published in Great Britain in 2001 by Falklands Conservation
1 Princes Avenue, Finchley, London N3 2DA.

Web Site: www.falklandsconservation.com

UK Registered Charity: 1073859

ISBN: 0-9538371-1-4

Copyright © 2001
Falklands Conservation (text)
Jeremy Smith (maps)
Copyright in the photographs remains with the individual
photographers

Disclaimer: The information given in this publication on behalf of
Falklands Conservation is believed to be correct, but accuracy is
not guaranteed and the information does not obviate the need to
make further enquiries as appropriate.

Designed by: Quetzal Communications, Old Basing, Hampshire, UK.
Printed in Hong Kong by The Hanway Press Ltd
Printed on chlorine-free paper from a sustainable source.

DEDICATION

To Lars-Eric Lindblad,
the pioneer of
expedition cruising

*Lars-Eric Lindblad and Roddy Napier in West Point Garden,
January 8th 1994*

Born in Stanley in 1972, Deborah (Debbie) Summers was educated first in the Falkland Islands and later at Peter Symonds College in Winchester, England. She returned to the Falkland Islands to work in 1996 after graduating with honours in Leisure Management and Tourism at Leeds University, where her dissertation dealt with the perceptions of cruise ship visitors to Stanley.

Taking advantage of the Falkland Islands Government two-year post-graduate training programme, Debbie worked for the Falkland Islands Tourist Board, Falklands Conservation, Falkland Islands Museum and National Trust as well as two London-based public relations companies on secondment. She has twice represented the Falkland Islands Government at British political party conferences and the Tourist Board at major promotional events in Britain and South America. Debbie has been employed by Falklands Conservation investigating cruise ship tourism for over two years and before beginning the not inconsiderable task of researching and writing this guide, was sponsored by the Falkland Islands Development Corporation to undertake an extended study on the conduct of cruise ship tourism in the Falklands, with special reference to the outer islands.

Passionate about her homeland, its people, traditions and wildlife, Debbie typifies a new generation of Falkland Islanders, which with its self-confidence, education and independence of thought augurs well for the future of this very special place.

FALKLANDS CONSERVATION – Working for Falkland Islands Wildlife

Falklands Conservation is the charity that takes action for nature in the Falkland Islands. For three years we have worked to promote environmentally sensitive tourism and this guide is the result. We want to make sure that the huge number of visitors who come to the Falklands get the very best from their experience but also that they have clear guidelines to ensure that no harm is done to the wonderful wildlife so many come to enjoy.

Wildlife has been in trouble here since the Falkland Islands were first settled in the 18th century. Seals and penguins were slaughtered in their hundreds of thousands for their skins and oil. Grazing by sheep damaged the native vegetation. Only one fifth of the native tussac grass cover remains. The introduction of rats has wiped out thousands of burrowing and ground nesting birds. Today the development of an offshore oil industry and a large commercial fishery in Falkland waters pose grave potential threats to our spectacular seabird populations. Changes in agriculture encourage non-native introductions and new roads improve access to previously remote areas therefore increasing pressure. Falklands Conservation is working closely with these industries and local people to try and ensure future developments are carried out sensitively.

Falklands Conservation plays an active role in protecting the Islands' environment. We rescue oiled seabirds, undertake studies of the seabird populations including research into diet, distribution at sea, and satellite tracking of penguins and albatrosses. We are mapping the Islands flora and have established a national Herbarium and are replanting areas of eroded tussac grass. We conducted a census of the breeding population of the remarkable striated caracara in 1997-1998 and have initiated a programme to eradicate rats from key offshore islands. We run a nature club for young Islanders and involve the community in beach clean-ups and other practical conservation

projects. Falklands Conservation owns 17 island nature reserves where Falklands wildlife is able to thrive in undisturbed sanctuaries. We publish regular newsletters for members, scientific reports and occasional guide books.

Although Falklands Conservation receives grants from the Falkland Islands Government and local businesses we heavily rely on public donations and subscriptions to carry out most of our projects. We invite every visitor to support this vital work by becoming a member. This will keep you in touch with the Islands and at the same time directly help protect Falklands wildlife for generations to come. We greatly appreciate any donations, large or small; they make a real difference.

We sincerely hope you enjoy your visit to the Falkland Islands, seeing its incredible wildlife, soaking up the atmosphere and using this guide.

Becky Ingham
Conservation Officer
Falklands Conservation

FALKLAND ISLANDS TOURIST BOARD

It is probable that more people cross the Brooklyn Bridge into Manhattan each morning than have ever visited the Falkland Islands since time began. However, the growth of cruise ship visits to the Falklands and the increased access provided by a commercial air link have meant that what seemed previously to be a small exclusive club has suddenly grown much bigger.

The Falkland Islands welcome the opportunity this gives to share something of our way of life and surroundings with visitors from all over the globe. However, with greater visitor numbers comes a greater responsibility to ensure that everything possible is done to protect the environment which makes the Falklands so attractive to visitors. We at the Falkland Islands Tourist Board are happy to share in this responsibility and it is for this reason that we are proud to have enabled Debbie Summers to carry out the study of visitor impacts on wildlife sites which led ultimately to the writing of this excellent and long-overdue publication: A Visitor's Guide to the Falkland Islands.

Here in this land of wide horizons and big skies we are keen not to have to constrain our many wildlife sites with fences, ropes, warning signs and all the prescriptive paraphernalia of outdoor zoos. The sheer volume of visitors has regrettably made this necessary in a few places close to Stanley, but it remains our earnest wish, wherever possible, to

preserve and present the landscape in as pristine a form as possible.

The achievement of this task of combining the presentation of the rich natural environment of the Islands with its preservation has relied in the past in great measure on the efforts of enlightened landowners and the high quality of the leaders employed by the majority of expedition cruise ships. Elsewhere, Debbie Summers has acknowledged the help she has received from both groups in putting together this attractive and informative guide; they, I am sure, will have reason in the future to thank her and Falklands Conservation for making this difficult but necessary task so much easier.

The Falkland Islands Tourist Board has great pleasure in commending A Visitor's Guide to the Falkland Islands, to everyone, not just those arriving by cruise ship, for whom it was originally intended. For visitors from abroad and residents alike, I am sure that this guide with its many beautiful illustrations and detailed maps, will prove to be an essential purchase.

John A T Fowler
Manager
Falkland Islands Tourist Board

CONTENTS

Falkland Islands Countryside Code . . . . .inside front cover

Map of the Falkland Islands showing site locations . . . . .inside back cover

Falklands Conservation *Becky Ingham* 5

Falkland Islands Tourist Board *John A T Fowler* 7

Foreword *Sven-Olof Lindblad* 9

Acknowledgements 11

A VISITOR'S GUIDE TO THE FALKLAND ISLANDS 12

THE FALKLAND ISLANDS – An expedition leader's perspective *Allan White* 15

PHOTOGRAPHY IN THE FALKLAND ISLANDS *Tony Chater* 16

A BRIEF HISTORY 19

THE FALKLAND ISLANDS PEOPLE 23

ARRIVAL BY SEA – Berkeley Sound – Port William – Stanley Harbour 25

STANLEY 28

FALKLANDS FACTS 34

THE GUIDE

BLEAKER ISLAND 36

CARCASS ISLAND 40

GEORGE AND BARREN ISLANDS 46

GYPSY COVE 48

KIDNEY COVE 52

NEW ISLAND 56
New Island North Nature Reserve   *Tony Chater* 58
New Island South Wildlife Reserve   *Ian J Strange* 64

PORT HOWARD 68

SAUNDERS ISLAND 70

SEA LION ISLAND 76

STEEPLE JASON   *Tony Chater* 82

VOLUNTEER POINT 86

WEDDELL ISLAND 92

WEST POINT ISLAND 94

Glossary of terms 100

Further reading 101

Useful addresses 102

Checklist of fauna and flora mentioned in the text 103

Photographic credits 108

FOREWORD *by Sven-Olof Lindblad*

My father, Lars-Eric Lindblad, brought the first expedition ship passengers to the Falkland Islands in 1968. Lindblad Expeditions continues to this day to bring people to the Islands and many thousands of other visitors now arrive to explore dramatic landscapes and gaze at the spectacular wildlife.

The very nature of the Falkland Islands makes them ideal for exploration by sea, consisting of over 700 small islands, fragments of our planet which remain relatively unspoilt by humanity. Here you can witness the grace and beauty of the albatross, marvel at the gusto of the rockhopper penguin as it battles the elements, and listen to the raucous voice of the fur seal echoing off the rock cliffs of New Island. It is a remote wilderness away from the hectic pace of modern life.

No surprise that the Falkland Islands have become such a popular destination and that this popularity has brought some potentially damaging pressures to the fragile environment. This most welcome and timely publication sets out clear advice to ensure that the impact from tourism is kept to a minimum. At the same time it offers a wealth of information for visitors describing both the wildlife of the major sites and the fascinating stories of the Islanders who have made this very special place their home. Stepping ashore with this guide in their pocket will surely enhance the experience of every visitor to the Falkland Islands.

ACKNOWLEDGEMENTS

This guide could not have got off the ground without the help of the following people. Very special thanks must go to Allan White, Robin and Anne Woods and to John Fowler for their support, advice and invaluable contributions throughout the whole period of working on this book. Also, I owe a special debt to Jeremy Smith for producing the site maps, to Rob Still for overseeing design and production, to Annie Gisby for proof reading and to Klemens Pütz. A special mention must be made of Kevin Schafer who donated many of his stunning photographs for inclusion in the Guide.

I am also very grateful to the following for their help and advice: Samantha Allanson-Bailey, Mike Bingham, David Broughton, Ann Brown, Jane Cameron, Sukey Cameron, Ross Chaloner, Andrea Clausen, Peter and Jennifer Clement, Richard Cockwell, John Croxall, Emma Edwards, the Falkland Islands Company, Debs Ford, David Gray, Alan Henry, Nic Huin, Becky Ingham, Anne Johnston, Gordon Liddle, Cindy May, Jim McAdam, Bob McDowall, Hay Miller, Jo Morrison, Mike and Sue Morrison, Ron Naveen, the Penguin News Team, Nick Rendell, Leona Roberts, John Smith, Joan Spruce, Philip Stone, Ian Strange, Sulivan Shipping Services Ltd and Synergy Information Systems.

I would like to acknowledge with many thanks all those who have submitted written material including Tony Chater, Tom Eggeling, Tony Smith, Ian Strange and Mandy Shepherd for her delightful sketches.

Photographs have been kindly provided by the following: Olle Carlsson, John Carr, Falkland Islands Museum and National Trust Collection, Hugh Harrop, Nigel Hawks, Nic Huin, Anna King, Gordon Langsbury, Mike Morrison, Roddy Napier, Peter Nightingale, Peter Pepper, Todd Pusser, the Seabirds At Sea Team (Andy Black, Keith Gillon, Richard White), Ian Strange, Andy Swash and Allan White.

Many Islanders, particularly landowners, have given valuable information on the social history and wildlife for each site. Without this help, provided in the form of photographs, data, memories and anecdotes, and the general support and encouragement from the community, this guide could not have been produced. Apologies to anyone who may have been accidentally missed out; it is not intentional.

Falklands Conservation wish to gratefully acknowledge the financial support provided for this publication by the Falkland Islands Government and Stanley Services Ltd.

Ancient and modern: a road cuts across the stone runs, a famous Falklands geological phenomenon

A VISITOR'S GUIDE TO THE FALKLAND ISLANDS

The Falkland Islands are among the few places left that can truly be described as "off the beaten track". Most first-timers to the Islands are pleasantly surprised. The temperate climate (with occasional strong winds) coupled with breathtaking scenery, a fascinating way of life and abundant wildlife all contribute.

THE GUIDE

Fifteen sites are described, all currently visited by cruise vessels. There are four future sites briefly described which are hoping to attract the cruise industry. The introductory map shows the location of each place within the Falkland archipelago. The text outlines history, geology, possible landing places, hikes and the historic sites and wildlife likely to be seen. English names are used for flora and fauna in the text. A checklist of all species mentioned, with their English and scientific names, is included. There are photographs and specially drawn maps. Most of these tourist sites are privately owned and the unique maps contain information added personally by landowners that you will not find in print anywhere else. All measurements are given in imperial and metric units. The 'features' column for each site provides site-specific information and the 'pointers' column has specific reference to the Falkland Islands Countryside Code.

CLIMATE

The Falkland Islands have a temperate oceanic climate and pollution-free skies, with stunning sunrises and sunsets providing wonderful photographic opportunities. Average daytime temperatures range from 36°F (2°C) in July to 48°F (9°C) in January. The lowest recorded temperature was 12·5°F (-9·5°C) in July 1995 and the highest was 85°F (29·2°C) in January 1992. Rainfall is generally low at around 26 inches (650 mm) per annum and the wind is persistent, usually westerly, with an average speed of about 15 knots. Stanley is one of the wettest places in the Islands, due to the showers generated as damp, cool, westerly winds are forced to rise above the Wickham Heights whilst West Falkland and outlying islands enjoy more sunshine and higher temperatures. This might explain an old Falkland saying that 'The West is best'.

The Meteorological Office at Mount Pleasant Airfield is available for weather forecasts either verbally or by fax, telephone number: 73559. A recorded weather forecast is available on telephone number 32500.

FLORA AND FAUNA

The predominant vegetation of the Islands is oceanic heathland consisting of dwarf shrubs, coarse whitegrass and cushion plants. Tussac grass used to cover much of the mainland East and West Falkland coasts, but almost all has been destroyed through overgrazing and erosion. Today it survives mostly on uninhabited and ungrazed offshore islands where it provides a unique ecological niche and excellent habitat for many breeding birds, sea mammals and invertebrates. Altogether, 347 species of plants have been recorded growing wild in the Falklands, of which 171 are

native. Thirteen species are considered to be endemic and there is a good chance that you will see some of these during your visit.

All penguin population figures are taken from the Falklands Conservation Penguin Census 2000/2001 and are given as numbers of breeding pairs. There are no figures for Magellanic penguins as they nest in burrows and are very difficult to count. About 60 species of birds breed in the Falkland Islands and at least 150 more species occur as vagrants or non-breeding regular visitors. The vagrants are often species that breed in southern South America which are blown westwards when on spring or autumn migration. You may be lucky enough to see something unusual.

FOR YOUR SAFETY
In an Emergency
The following channels may prove useful when travelling through Falkland Islands waters; Royal Falkland Islands Police VHF 153·650 +Dup 1.6 and the 2 Metre Calling Channel VHF 145·500.

Sunburn
A high factor sun cream is advisable as, despite the low temperatures, ultra violet intensity is very high in the clear air. Combined with the drying effect of high winds, burn times can be as low as twenty minutes on a cloudless day. At times when the 'ozone hole' spreads northwards from Antarctica, the risk of burning and ultra violet-related damage to skin is even greater.

Cruise visitors on Leopard Beach, Carcass Island with Peale's dolphins offshore

Land Mines

There are 135 mined areas in the Falkland Islands (left from the 1982 Conflict) which cover an area of approximately 7·7sq miles (20sq km). Most of the minefields are near Stanley and some of the larger camp settlements and are very clearly fenced and marked. It is thought that approximately 25,000 to 30,000 mines were laid and to date an estimated 6,000 of these have been destroyed. The cost of removing the remaining mines using current technology could run to £50 million ($75 million). These mines are a tragic consequence of war, but ironically they now provide a unique haven for wildlife. More information and minefield maps can be obtained from the Joint Service Explosive Ordnance Disposal Operations Centre located opposite the Police Station in Stanley.

> **Please do not attempt to enter any minefields or remove minefield signs. It is a crime to do so. Penalties are severe, with fines in the region of £1000 ($1500).**

Risk of Fire

There is an extremely high fire risk due to the peaty ground, so please be extremely careful if smoking anywhere in the Islands. There is a no-smoking policy for some islands.

Respect for Wildlife

Never attempt to handle wildlife or disturb birds when nesting. Not only does this cause distress, it can leave chicks and eggs open to predation. Please do not put your hand into a penguin burrow. Penguins bite and burrows contain fleas, so you have been warned.

Falkland skuas, South American terns, red-backed hawks and striated caracaras may attack if you enter their territories. If you feel threatened, hold a stick above your head and leave the area.

Many coastal areas are undermined by Magellanic penguin burrows. Please take care when walking as you may destroy their homes or twist your ankle.

It is dangerous to get between a seal and the sea, especially if you have disturbed a large bull in tussac grass. They may appear cumbersome on land but they can move very quickly downhill.

FOR THE SAFETY OF BIRDS AND MAMMALS

When approaching wildlife, please stop at a sensible distance. The Falkland Islands Countryside Code indicates 20 ft (6 m). When wildlife shows signs of distress, you are too close. Wildlife will come and see you if you give them time and keep your distance. Southern giant petrels are particularly vulnerable to disturbance when nesting and you must stay at least 45 ft (13 m) away from these birds. Keep low and be as quiet as possible.

Avoid 'penguin highways' especially when the birds are feeding chicks. These traditional routes are used between the sea and the nest sites.

THE FALKLAND ISLANDS - An expedition leader's perspective

For many people, the Falklands is little more than "a place somewhere down south where Britain and Argentina fought a war". The truth is that beyond the well-known but tragic events of 1982, there lies a pristine and tranquil archipelago of incredible beauty, where nature thrives in abundance and variety. For most visitors, the Falklands is usually part of a cruise package that includes Antarctica and/or South America. However you travel, the Falklands will far exceed your expectations and become one of the highlights of your journey.

The show begins at sea as you approach the Islands. Albatrosses, petrels, shearwaters, and prions escort ships, riding the southern ocean winds with elegance and ease. This airborne parade is just a taste of what lies in store. The Falklands wildlife leaves everyone spellbound, especially photographers and bird-watchers who think they have died and gone to heaven. The Falklands provide up-close and personal encounters with some very rare and remarkably tame species, like the striated caracara. The Islands are also a stronghold for the beautiful black-browed albatross, which breeds in vast numbers on some islands.

Stanley, our small but colourful capital offers a range of growing services. Whether you decide to take a guided tour, or explore the tidy streets independently, you will find it a charming and friendly place. But it is outside Stanley, in remoter parts, that the real Falklands exists. An avian paradise of unparalleled beauty awaits, along with a handful of Island folk who live a unique lifestyle.

An excellent variety of landings are available on both East and West Falklands, with each site being very different in terms of scenery and wildlife. All sites offer superb hiking opportunities, and the chance to take in some of the Falklands' finest scenery. Most landings are wet, but one or two locations offer dry jetty landings for boats on all tides. Most wet landings are onto sandy beaches, with rocks being only an occasional obstacle. Keep your eyes open during boat transfers: you may find yourself in the company of dolphins.

The prevailing westerly winds are a dominant feature of the climate. Do not under-estimate the weather. Nowhere is more beautiful than the Falklands on a fine day, but be prepared for changeable conditions. Talk to the locals during island visits: they are keen observers of the weather. In extreme cases it may be necessary to terminate activities at more exposed sites, so cruise Expedition Leaders should know the location of any alternate landing sites and ensure everyone is familiar with their ship's recall procedures.

Don't forget the human factor. Island visits provide the chance to meet some wonderful characters, whose tales of Island life will greatly enhance your experience. The warmth and hospitality of these people is second to none. Whatever your interests, wildlife, scenery, hiking, people, geology, history, or just a passion for the rugged and remote, the Falklands has it all. Enjoy this beautiful corner of the world and please help us to look after it.

Allan White

PHOTOGRAPHY IN THE FALKLAND ISLANDS

Photographing this beautiful group of islands has given me a huge amount of pleasure during the last 25 years. This is a country of sweeping moorlands, big skies and seascapes. The air is so very clean that, on a clear day, you can see for extraordinary distances. But, because much of the land is low lying with no great mountains or native trees, and because there are relatively few people and buildings outside Stanley and Mount Pleasant Airport, it can be challenging to find that special subject.

Just getting to a lot of the more interesting places can be difficult in the extreme, even for those of us who live here. Only those outer islands which are inhabited can be reached by light aircraft and only during the last decade has there been the growth of a road network across East and West Falkland. However, for me by far the most interesting, traditional and natural way to travel here is that used by the earliest visitors to these shores. It is, of course, by way of the sea.

I have been on many sea voyages in this area and am pleased to see that the locations described in this site guide for sea-borne visitors offer the very finest opportunities for the photographer in the Falklands.

In these places you will find abundant wildlife amongst magnificent scenery. Many of the bird species, particularly the albatross and some of the penguins, are remarkably tame. But remember that this is their home and, like us, they need their own space to live in. The best pictures are always the ones where the subjects are behaving naturally. Try to move slowly and talk quietly. Keep a reasonable distance away 20 ft, (6 m) so as not to disturb the birds. If you find a convenient rock to sit on whilst at one of the penguin colonies (and if you stay still) the penguins will sometimes approach you and even nibble at your clothing.

The picturesque island farms and homesteads offer you a glimpse of a traditional way of life. Each settlement consists of a clutch of gaily-coloured buildings usually surrounded by a patchwork of bright green, sheep-holding paddocks, sited in a sheltered bay. They look well nestling amongst the buffs, greys, and olive greens of the moorland; a pleasing touch of order amid the random patterns of nature.

The people who live in these places are self-sufficient, weathered and welcoming in the way that people in remote areas often are. They are always willing to exchange stories and, of course, can provide you with copious local information.

Life is dominated by the wind and the sea so you will need to protect your camera gear against salt spray, particularly when travelling in the small boats from your ship to the shore. Small cameras of the "point and shoot" variety are safest in a ziplock plastic bag until you get onshore. Bring along a few spare bags in case they get torn or wet. Those

Tony Chater
New Island North
Nature Reserve

Kidney Island – stay low and quiet and the rockhoppers will come to you

people who like to carry more camera gear might be wise to invest in a "dry bag" which are available in most camera stores. It may be worthwhile to get one that has carrying straps so you can use it as a backpack. Beware of sand getting into your equipment (particularly tripods and monopods) when you are changing clothes or footwear on the landing beach. It can ruin your trip. Lastly beware of those remarkably tame hawks called striated caracaras or 'johnny rooks' who are both incurably inquisitive and insatiably acquisitive. To put it bluntly they will fly off with anything they can carry irrespective of how much you paid for it. Lens caps, film canisters, and sunglasses are their specialities but I have known them to take off with small cameras as well.

Bring enough film and spare batteries with you to last for the whole voyage. The range of both in Stanley can be very limited. Colour slide film is generally unavailable. I recommend Fuji or Kodak film with a speed of 50 or 100 ASA to give good colour and sharp resolution to your slides or prints. However, if you are prone to camera shake you may prefer to use a faster film with a rating of 200ASA.

If you have bought a new camera for this holiday it is a good idea to shoot off a couple of rolls of film and have them processed to make sure everything works properly before you leave home. Don't wait until you are going ashore in a force 9 gale before you decide to load your first roll! It may also be a good idea to bring the camera manual with you as there are no camera repair shops along the way.

You will all have your own preferences for the camera gear that you wish and are able to take on this trip. In most cases weight will be a major factor. Many of you will be content with a "point and shoot" model. These can give excellent results and are certainly easier to manage when you are leaping in and out of boats. For those people who, like me, prefer to go ashore armed with an arsenal of equipment I have the following suggestions based on personal experience:-

- One single lens reflex body or two if you are really serious and worried about breakdowns. *I use a Canon EOS 3.*
- A fast standard lens. *I use a 50mm f1.4 Canon AF*
- A wide angle zoom lens. *I use a 17-35mm f2.8 Canon AF*
- A telephoto zoom lens. *I use a 70-200mm f2.8 Canon AF with a 2x extender.*

Protect each of your lenses against dust, sand and salt with a UV filter and take something along to keep the filters clean. Lens cleaning tissues are best but a clean handkerchief will do. Failing that just turn your back on the crowd and give them a quick wipe with your tee shirt.

Take along a circular polarizing filter to enhance the colours and, in particular, the skies.

Tripods are heavy and awkward but I find them indispensable when shooting landscapes. I use a lightweight Gitzo G1228 mk2. It has a hook on it and if it's windy you can always hang something heavy from this to give added stability. If you use a tripod you will also need a cable release.

A lockable "Pelican" case is the best thing for protecting your gear in transit unless you plan to carry it as hand baggage.

If you plan to go ashore with a relatively small amount of gear I strongly recommend that you consider a waist pack (known as "bum bags" in Britain or "fanny packs" in the US). These are comfortable to wear and leave both your hands free for clambering about, particularly in and out of boats.

Having said all this the most important thing is to enjoy your holiday so have fun and I hope you have calm seas and plenty of sunshine.

A BRIEF HISTORY

About 400 million years ago the continents of the Southern Hemisphere all lay adjacent to each other, forming the giant super continent of Gondwanaland. The Falkland Islands were tucked in between the future south-east coast of Africa and part of what was to become Antarctica. As the larger masses, destined to become our present-day continents, gradually moved apart, several much smaller fragments were jostled between them; one of these was the Falklands continental block. It initially broke away from the south-east side of Africa and as its much larger neighbours separated, the small Falklands block was twisted around, rotating through almost 180 degrees. By about 150 million years ago it had been pushed up against the margin of the new South American continent.

Over the last 150 million years the Atlantic Ocean has opened up to create the familiar geography of today. The mid-ocean volcanic ridge eventually developed to the east of the rotated Falklands block and so the islands moved away from their African origins in the new-found embrace of South America. This earlier location lends support to the current interest in the exploratory work presently being carried out to locate possible diamonds and gold in the Falkland Islands.

Although it is likely that the Falkland Islands were sighted some years previously, the English navigator Captain John Davis is credited with the first confirmed sighting and accurate recording of their position on the 14th August 1592. Two years later another English captain, Sir Richard Hawkins, sighted the Islands and named them Hawkins Maydenlande. The first recorded landing was in January 1690 by Captain John Strong with his ship the *Welfare* who put into Bold Cove, near Port Howard on West Falkland, to replenish his ship with water. He then named the Sound which divides the two main islands, after Viscount Falkland who was Treasurer to the Admiralty.

Stanley has not always been the capital; until 1843 the seat of government was Port Louis, in the north-east of East Falkland. Port Louis, or Fort St Louis as it was originally called, was the earliest settlement in the Falklands, founded by the French in the 18th century. Louis Antoine de Bougainville was an idealistic young Frenchman who had fought in Canada and witnessed the loss of Quebec to the British in 1756. He dreamt of founding a new settlement for the Acadians who had been expelled from Canada to St. Malo and chose the uninhabited Falklands, thinking the new colony would be safe from harassment in such a remote place. He equipped an expedition and in 1764 successfully established a settlement of some 80 people at Port Louis.

However the French occupation of Port Louis was not destined to last long. The British established a settlement at Port Egmont on Saunders Island off West Falkland in 1765 and were surprised and more than a little dismayed to discover the French

Stanley Harbour in the 19th Century

settlement when sailing around the Islands in December 1766. Although relations between the two communities in the Falklands were fairly cordial, settlers were drawn into the complicated web of European politics. Spain objected to the French settlement in a land that she claimed as a dependency of her South American dominions. France was reluctant to risk either upsetting Spain or provoking war with England and the French were persuaded to relinquish their claim by the payment of a sum equal to £25,000 ($38,000) to them by Spain. The British settlement on Saunders Island was evacuated under pressure from Spanish warships in 1767 but was reinstated by an act of restitution by Spain in 1771. However, in 1774 Britain decided that it was uneconomic to maintain this settlement and the small garrison was withdrawn in 1776, leaving behind a lead plaque proclaiming the dominion of King George III over the Falkland Islands. The Spaniards abandoned Port Louis in 1811 and for the next few years the Islands had no settled population. Then in 1826, Louis Vernet, a businessman of German extraction from the River Plate, set up a successful fisheries and cattle business.

In 1831 an incident over sealing rights, which involved a number of American vessels, resulted in the arrival of the US warship *Lexington*, which almost destroyed the settlement by gunfire. Two years later Britain re-established her presence in the Falklands by resettling and rebuilding Port Louis, which thrived until the decision to remove the seat of government to Stanley in 1843.

LINKS WITH SOUTH GEORGIA

South Georgia and the South Sandwich Islands has been a UK Overseas Territory in its own right since 1985. Before 1985, it was a dependency of the Falkland Islands. The Governor of the Falkland Islands is also the Commissioner for South Georgia and the South Sandwich Islands (SGSSI).

The Falkland Islands Government maintained a small administration team on South Georgia until 1969. During this period, links between the Falklands and South Georgia were very strong and many Falkland Islanders worked there, both as government employees and, up to 1965, in the whaling industry. The Government of SGSSI now administers sustainable fisheries and a flourishing tourism industry with a marine officer appointed from the Falklands. He/she is supported by the British Antarctic Survey, who also carry out applied fishery science on behalf of the South Georgia Government and form the majority of the population.

South Georgia has the greatest concentrations of Antarctic and sub-Antarctic wildlife on earth seen against a backdrop of fabulous glaciated mountain scenery. The South Georgia Museum at Grytviken (set up in 1992) is a must for visitors and celebrates the industrial heritage, exploration and wildlife of the region.

Early morning – Three riders just off for beef

NOTICE TO MARINERS.
(No 8.)

FALKLAND ISLANDS.   FIXED LIGHT ON CAPE PEMBROKE.

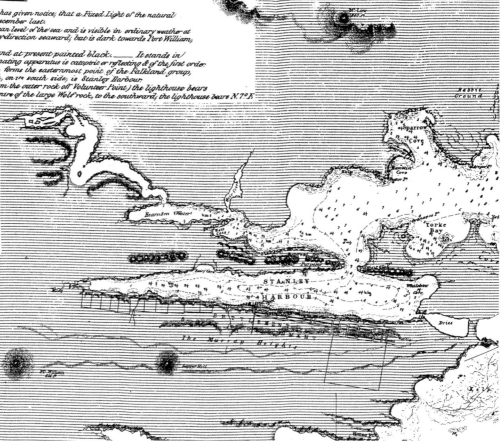

The Colonial Government at the Falkland Islands has given notice, that a Fixed Light of the natural colour was established on Cape Pembroke on the first of December last.

The light stands at a height of 110 feet above the mean level of the sea and is visible in ordinary weather at a distance of 14 miles. It shows a bright fixed light in every direction seaward, but is dark towards Port William, between the bearings of N.W. ½ N. and West.

The tower is 60 feet high; it is circular, and of iron, and at present painted black.___ It stands in lat. 51°40'42" S., 57°41'48" West of Greenwich. The illuminating apparatus is catoptric or reflecting & of the first order.

Cape Pembroke, on which a beacon has hitherto stood, forms the easternmost point of the Falkland group, and also the south headland of Port William, within which, on its south side, is Stanley Harbour.

From the Uranie Rock (which lies east one mile from the centre of Volunteer Point) the lighthouse bears S. 13°E or S. by E. ½ E. nearly, distant 9½ miles. From the centre of the large Wolf rock, to the southward, the lighthouse bears N.7°E.

A vessel entering Port William will leave the light on the port hand, and the Master should be careful to observe that, as the flood tide sets strongly to the northward and the ebb to the southward in passing Cape Pembroke, he should not pass between this Cape and the Seal Rocks (which lie north-east of it about ½ mile) unless the ship is under steam or has a good commanding breeze: in light winds or much swell, it is better to pass outside.

(All bearings are Magnetic.   Var 16¾°E. in 1856.)

By Command of their Lordships,
(Signed)   **JOHN WASHINGTON**,
Hydrographer.

Hydrographic Office, Admiralty, London,
5th February, 1856.

STANLEY is a Free Port.___ Good Water, Fresh Provisions, Vegetables, and Supplies of all sorts are procurable. Ships can also be repaired.

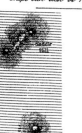

Cape Pembroke Lighthouse.
painted in white and red bands
110 feet high.

Falkland Islanders:
Billy Poole using hand
shears (far left);
A Falkland wedding
long ago (above);
Mrs Macaskill riding
side saddle (left)

THE FALKLAND ISLANDS PEOPLE

Fifty years on, the following description of Islanders still holds good:

'The Falkland Islanders come of a hardy stock, content with a decent life of personal achievement, proud of their own strength of character, their origins, and their family ties…of such outstanding qualifications and hardiness for work, in as often as not, the harshest of weather in this distant Colony of the British Commonwealth.'

F.I.C. Centenary Booklet, 1951

Falkland Islanders are predominantly of British stock. Historically, recruitment for farm workers was often concentrated in the rural areas of Scotland and southern England. There are also a number of families of Scandinavian origin within the population, their forebears having remained in the Falklands after being shipwrecked during the 18th and 19th centuries.

The remoteness of the Falkland Islands before 1982 resulted in a community that through necessity had developed a remarkable adaptability. This, since 1982, has enabled them to cope calmly and astutely with a wide and dramatic range of changes to their lifestyle.

Islanders living in remote parts of the Falkland Islands today sometimes appear isolated. While on one side of the kitchen you may still find a peat burning stove, often on the other side will be installed up to date computer and communications equipment with the owners more than able to hold forth on the latest international developments and benefits from information technology. The World Wide Web could have been invented particularly with Falkland Islanders in mind.

Often underestimated by the outside world, Islanders are now proving their intellectual capability by qualifying in many professions that were previously the province of imported expertise.

Frank Smith with the Nancy in the background

Shepherd gang c. 1890s

23

Drawn on Stone by A R Grave, from a Sketch by Lt Lowcay R N.

M&N Hanhart, Lith Printers, 64 Charlotte St Rathbone P...

VIEW OF THE HARBOR OF PORT LOUIS~BERKLEY SOUND, EAST FALKLAND.

HMS Sparrow *at anchor off Port Louis c. 1838/39*

ARRIVAL BY SEA – Berkeley Sound – Port William – Stanley Harbour

When sailing from the north towards the Islands' capital, Stanley, you will pass the wide entrance to Berkeley Sound. At the head of this large inlet is the tiny settlement of Port Louis, which was the former capital of the Falklands, originally founded by the French in 1764. It sometimes took as long as two days for a sailing ship to traverse Berkeley Sound, beating against the prevailing westerly wind. This is one of the reasons why the British Admiralty recommended in the 1840's that the capital be moved to Stanley, with its more easily accessible harbour. Berkeley Sound is now used for transhipping squid by vessels engaged in the fishing industry.

As you continue the passage to Stanley, Cape Pembroke lighthouse comes into view, prominent at the end of a long low spit of land. This splendid traditional Victorian lighthouse was first lit in 1855 and remained in service until the war of 1982. It was built to warn incoming ships of the treacherous reefs of rock just off the coast, in particular the small but lethal Billy Rock which we know to have claimed at least ten ships. Today, an electronic beacon performs the navigational aid function of the lighthouse.

After turning into Stanley's outer harbour, Port William, the low cliffs visible on your right hand side surround the small cove of Hell's Kitchen in which the South Atlantic Ocean froths and roars during great storms.

On travelling further into Port William, Sparrow Cove lies on the northern side where Brunel's famous steamship, the SS *Great Britain*, lay beached as a breakwater from the late 1930s until 1970, when she was returned to Bristol in the United Kingdom to be restored to her original elegance.

On the southern shore of Port William is the great expanse of Yorke Bay, a wonderful example of a Falklands beach, with merging sand dunes rising behind the white sand beach. Unfortunately, since 1982 it has been a minefield and access is forbidden. Gypsy Cove, at its western end, is home to Stanley's nearest penguin colony. Here, Magellanic penguins, known locally as 'jackass' from their donkey-like braying, can be found. On the high ground behind the Cove is a redundant World War II Vickers gun, installed for the defence of the outer harbour against the threat of German or Japanese attack. Due to the strategic importance of the Islands at this time, a large garrison of British Forces was based in Stanley.

Photographers should look out for the striking panorama of mountains and hills, visible directly ahead. Then the ship turns to slip through the Narrows to enter Stanley Harbour. By the beacon on the eastern side of the Narrows is an iron chain, the only reminder of a steel net which could be pulled across the harbour entrance as a deterrent to enemy ships entering in the hours of darkness during World War I.

Cape Pembroke lighthouse from the sea

A squid jigging vessel

Brown-hooded gulls can be seen on the approach to the harbour all year round. Adult bird in spring plumage (above); birds in winter plumage (below)

This snug anchorage is sheltered on all sides by high ground. The town of Stanley is located on the southern shore and faces the once very important but now derelict, Naval Fuel Depot on the northern shore at the Camber. After 1982, the Falklands Interim Port and Storage System (FIPASS) was constructed to the east of the town to cope with increasing calls by merchant and fishing vessels. Although unsightly, it is of vital importance to the economy of the Islands.

For some visitors, the most fascinating aspect of the inner harbour is the presence of so many remains of the once mighty maritime trade which flourished between about 1848 and 1870 on the Cape Horn route between Europe and the Americas. Many examples of wooden ship construction in the 19th century by Britain, the USA and Canada can be seen along the waterfront. Slowly but inexorably these hulks, some the only remaining examples of their type in the world today, are going to crumble and break up. On the north side of the harbour the names of guard ships of the Royal Navy for the Falkland Islands are set out in white stones to record vessels of a bygone era.

Entering Stanley Harbour

History in the harbour: the hulks of the Egeria *and the* William Shand *at FIC East Jetty with the* Snowsquall *and the steamer SS* Falkland *moored alongside (top); the* Lady Elizabeth *in her heyday (right); the* Jhelum *lying off Sulivan House on the western part of Stanley (far right)*

STANLEY

STANLEY

The view to the west of Stanley harbour is dominated by mountains and hills, with Mount Longdon and Mount Tumbledown lying north and south respectively, of the twin peaks of Two Sisters. The highest point on the horizon is Mount Kent, which at 1,504 ft (458 m), lies some 12 miles (19 km) from the town beyond Moody Valley. These peaks are now perpetuated in battle honours of units from the British Forces, who fought and liberated the Islands from Argentine occupation in 1982.

The town was established on the south shore of Jackson Harbour as Stanley harbour was then called, in the early 1840's. A major reason for the siting of the town here was the abundance of peat fuel in the surrounding area and another was the plentiful freshwater supply from the nearby Moody Brook, at the western head of the harbour. However, the greatest advantage of this site was a snug harbour easily accessible by sailing vessels.

Lieutenant Governor Richard Clement Moody was assigned to locate the site and begin the construction of the new town. By December 1843 work had started on the first buildings and by the winter of 1846, streets were laid out and the essential buildings had been completed. The new town of Stanley had begun to take shape. The kit houses, built by military pensioners, are still in good order and occupied to this day on Pioneer Row and Drury Street in the centre of the town.

On the high ground south of the town lies Stanley Common with its white grass plains. This extends east as far as Hookers Point, bordering the dramatic Surf Bay, which itself acts as an isthmus linking Cape Pembroke peninsula to east Stanley.

Isolation and the weather conditions made life hard. The old section of the cemetery is a unique record of the early pioneering days when whole families were struck down with what were then fatal epidemics.

Stanley waterfront c. 1915

Curiously it was the discovery of gold in California that put Stanley on its feet. Long before the construction of the Panama Canal the rush to the gold fields took prospectors and their families by sea, round Cape Horn and north to San Francisco. By the time many of these ships had reached the Falkland Islands they were in need of water, repairs and provisions. Moody and his men were able to provide these facilities with no competition because Stanley was the nearest port of refuge to Cape Horn. The only survivor in the world today of a vessel that actually took part in the Gold Rush of 1849 is the *Vicar of Bray,* the hull of which forms the jetty head at Goose Green. The opening of the Panama Canal in 1914 and the advent of steam taking over from sail brought to a close the great shipping boom which had benefited Stanley so much.

The sealers and whalers were a transient population who visited the Falkland Islands seasonally. The whalers would rest up and refit their ships in the snug harbours of West Falkland during the southern winter, then head south again in the austral summer to continue whaling until they had a full cargo of oil. The sealers and penguin hunters were actually based in the Islands, ruthlessly destroying colonies, exploiting penguins for oil and seals for both oil and pelts. In the latter half of the 19th century sealers used the town to restock with provisions and their carousing gave Stanley a dubious reputation.

Towards the end of the 19th century the emerging town was almost destroyed by the very thing that the settlers were reliant on: peat, the only source of fuel, vital for cooking and heating and essential for survival. In the early hours of 30th November 1878, the wet and unstable peat in the cuttings along the ridge above Stanley could hold back no longer. It slipped downwards in a thick lumpy slurry through the town, surrounding and isolating houses, cutting off any movement between the east and west ends of the town. Eight years later a second disastrous peat slip occurred. This time the liquid peat flowed faster, wrecking several houses in its path and killing one child and an old man.

Stanley continued to prosper on the maritime trade until the end of the 19th century when steam had obviously come to stay. The town then reverted to a supportive role, providing the infrastructure for the growing sheep farming industry that developed into the main source of revenue for the Falklands until the 1980's.

During those 80 years there were long periods of very gradual progress punctuated by the extremely eventful times of involvement in two world wars and regular visits of research vessels and warships of the Royal Navy. Supplies were brought in from Britain on the eagerly awaited quarterly charter vessel. This and the

Governor Richard Clement Moody, Governor of The Falkand Islands 1842-1848

The waterfront of Stanley showing, from left to right; Hambledon House, Christ Church Cathedral, the Whalebone Arch, FIC West Store and the vessel AK Ilen

monthly steamer to Montevideo were the main means of contact with the outside world until the introduction of an air link to Argentina in the early 1970's. Before then, the visitor would have found Stanley as it had been described by the Colonial Secretary in 1933;

> '...*A final impression ...on a clear day after rain will be one of fresh washed roads and red roofed houses nestling snug under the lee of the protective slope under which it was built, with the peat reek rising softly pungent in a tonic air...*'

Indeed, twenty years ago the town was much as Ernest Shackleton the great Antarctic explorer had encountered in 1916 with '*the graveyard at one end and the slaughterhouse at the other*'.

The last two decades of the 20th century illustrate a remarkable story of activity and progress in the Islands of which Stanley was the hub. Invasion, occupation and liberation in 1982 were followed by rapid development, most notably the establishment of the Falklands fishing regime and the exploratory drilling for oil. This (along with the de-population of the countryside) has caused the town to double in size with the latest growth concentrated towards the eastern end of the harbour, stretching the town's boundary even further.

You do not have to go out of the town to enjoy the outstanding wildlife the Islands have to offer. Southern giant petrels often fly close to the shoreline, keeping up with local residents driving along the front road. The endemic Falkland steamer ducks abound on the shorelines while kelp gulls

Jubilee Villas

can often be seen flying up in the air, dropping mussels on to the roads, so that the shells crack allowing them to eat the contents. Dolphin gulls are also numerous in the Stanley area. The less obvious but frequent visitors to the Stanley area are black-crowned night herons, red-backed hawks and peregrine falcons. Turkey vultures are regularly seen on top of any prominent building. In the harbour you may see Peale's and Commerson's dolphins during the journey from your ship to the shore. By the Falkland Islands Company jetty southern sea lions can sometimes be seen basking in the sunlight on the wrecks. Both rock and king cormorants are regularly seen on the wreck opposite the West Store and on the end of the public jetty. Many pairs of upland geese frequent Victory Green pecking at the green grass. Vehicles often have to give them the right of way. Smaller birds to be seen include the Falkland thrush, the red breasted long-tailed meadowlark, black-chinned siskins (particularly around the conifers in Government House garden) and introduced house sparrows.

The native vegetation found on the outskirts of the town is either dwarf shrub heath dominated by diddle-dee, grassland dominated by the straw coloured whitegrass, or dense stands of high,

glossy leafed, tall fern. In spring the heathlands are studded by the delicate, white flowers of the pale maiden. Stanley itself has a rich non-native flora, the vast majority being European in origin, reflecting the long historical and social ties with Britain. Notable non-natives include the orange-flowered fox-and-cubs which makes a striking contrast to the rest of the flora and fox-tail barley, the silky flower heads of which fringe the harbour in mid-summer.

Aerial view of Stanley East from the northwest (below); signpost erected by military personnel after the 1982 conflict (right)

Views of Stanley

This page: The 1982 war memorial (below);
Government House (right); Christ Church
Cathedral and Whalebone Arch (far right)

Facing page: A typical Falkland house (top left);
Fitzroy Road, looking towards the Wickham
Heights (top right); an aerial view of Stanley,
Port William and Cape Pembroke (below)

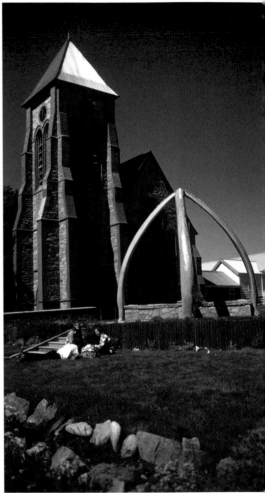

FALKLANDS FACTS

- Stanley was named after Edward Stanley 14th Earl of Derby who was the British Secretary of State for the Colonies at the time the capital was founded.

- The economy of the Islands is based on income from the sale of fishing licences. Investment income, agriculture, tourism and services are the other principal contributors to the economy and employment. Potential offshore oil reserves may provide an additional source of income in the future.

- In the last five years, 113 new homes have been built, demonstrating the rapid growth of the town.

- The Falkland Islands has a comprehensive health service funded by the Falkland Islands Government. The health service has 90 staff and the hospital contains 32 beds.

- Stanley secondary school (Falkland Islands Community School) cost £14 million ($21.5 million) when it was built in 1990. The Falklands have a policy of maintaining class size at less than 30 pupils and there are currently 46 Falkland Island students on courses of higher or further education in Britain. Stanley schools have 370 pupils and there are 29 pupils living in the Camp.

- The recently constructed Jetty Centre provides information for visitors.

- Britannia House Museum contains wide-ranging displays telling the story of a community which began with a cattle industry, then had a long period of maritime activity linked with sheep farming. It shows how the community was affected by two world wars, and then invaded in 1982. The charm and informality of this museum allows you to rummage and discover fascinating curiosities from restored mechanical musical instruments to carefully prepared skulls of some of the world's least known cetaceans.

- The Falkland Islands are self-governing except for areas of foreign affairs and defence. Eight councillors are elected every four years to the Legislative Council.

- Food and lodging is catered for by an impressive selection of hotels, guest houses, restaurants, cafés and pubs.

- Retail outlets scattered all around Stanley stock most essentials as well as souvenirs and local art and crafts. It is worth exploring away from the main road.

- International communication by telephone and internet is available at Cable and Wireless and the Hard Disk Café.

- The Falkland Islands Government Air Service operates Britten-Norman Islander aircraft out of Stanley to airstrips throughout the Islands.

THINGS YOU MAY NOT KNOW ABOUT THE FALKLAND ISLANDS

- Apart from the Mount Pleasant military complex, the total population in 2001 was 2,491. 1,989 in Stanley, 502 in the Camp.

- The Falkland Islands do not have any McDonald's.

- The total land area is 4,700 sq miles (12,200 sq km) and from east to west the broadest point is about 155 miles (250 km).

- The highest point is Mount Usborne 2,312 ft (705 m) on East Falkland.

- The greatest of all naturalists, Charles Darwin, visited the Islands in March to April 1833 and 1834. Despite appalling weather and living conditions, he collected data on the geology, fauna and flora of the Falklands which influenced his later work on evolution.

- For over 100 years, peat (or turf) has been the main fuel for heating and cooking. In recent years peat has been overtaken almost completely by kerosene or diesel for heating and bottled gas or electricity for cooking.

- The largest sea trout caught weighed 22lbs 12½ ounces (10·3 kg), (2½ oz (71 gm) heavier than the UK record. Incidentally, it was caught by a woman.

- The most popular form of transport is the 4 wheel drive vehicle, with a total of 1,111 in the Islands, mainly due to the amount of overland driving. The total road length in the islands is 248 miles (398·5 km) and there are no traffic lights.

- The total revenue from the Falkland Islands Fishery 1999/2000 was £25 million ($38.5 million).

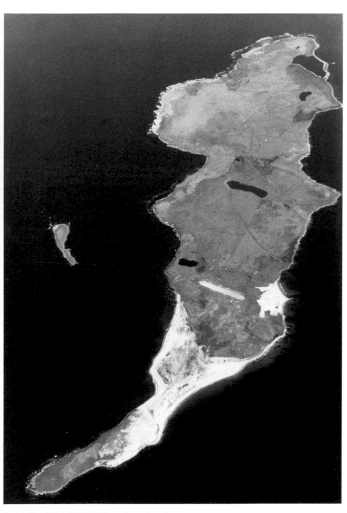

Aerial view of Sea Lion Island from the northeast

THE GUIDE

Key to the maps

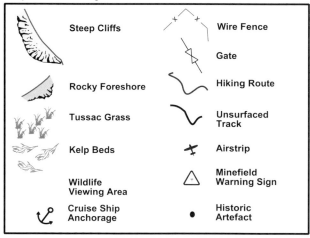

Steep Cliffs	Wire Fence
Rocky Foreshore	Gate
Tussac Grass	Hiking Route
Kelp Beds	Unsurfaced Track
Wildlife Viewing Area	Airstrip
Cruise Ship Anchorage	Minefield Warning Sign
	Historic Artefact

BLEAKER ISLAND

FEATURES

▸ Three species of penguin (rockhopper, Magellanic, gentoo). The occasional king penguin is present in the gentoo colonies

▸ A large king cormorant colony

▸ Waterfowl on Big Pond

▸ Sandy Bay and the Long Gulch area

Black-necked swans on Big Pond

INTRODUCTION

Bleaker Island was originally known as Long Island and Breaker Island and is in fact far from bleak. The island is 5,115 acres (2,070 ha) and its varied coastline includes great lengths of inviting white sandy beaches separated by sheltered coves. It lies close to the south-east coast of East Falkland and acts as a tide-break protecting Adventure Sound. It is long and thin, never more than 2 miles (3·2 km) wide and in many places is almost severed by heavy indentations created by the sea. Although Bleaker Island is just a 'stone's throw' from the mainland, the landing site at Sandy Bay is over 10 miles (16 km) from East Falkland.

In 1871 a visiting warship, HMS *Reindeer*, recorded that the whole of Bleaker Island was fringed with tussac and that wild pigs were the sole inhabitants. A further report by the local newspaper stated that in 1888 five vaults were discovered in the south-western corner of Sandy Bay opposite the anchorage to the westward of the two Sandy Bay islands. The origin of these vaults remains a mystery to this day and although it has always been assumed that they were graves, it appears more likely that they were built as food storage sites by sealers or penguin hunters. These reports are clear evidence of early habitation by sealers or other sailors.

Driftwood Point on East Falkland lies only half a mile (800 m) from Cassard Point, Bleaker's southern

Arthur Cobb, third from left who lived on the island until the mid-1920s

tip, across the Bleaker Jump. In days gone by a dinghy was rowed across this narrow stretch of water to pick up visiting farm managers, doctors, teachers and clergy, who arrived on horseback from the nearest settlement, North Arm, situated some 20 miles (32 km) to the west (see map on inside back cover).

The low silhouette of the Island and its neighbours may well account for a number of shipwrecks over the years. The *Cassard*, a French steel barque built in 1899, was bound from Cardiff to Sydney with a cargo of grain, when she was wrecked at the southern point of Bleaker Island in July 1906. During the next 20 years another four ships were lost at Bleaker Island.

BLEAKER ISLAND : 52°12'S 58°51'W (Settlement)   Ownership: Mike and Phyl Rendell   Size: 5,115 acres (2,070 ha)   Population: 2

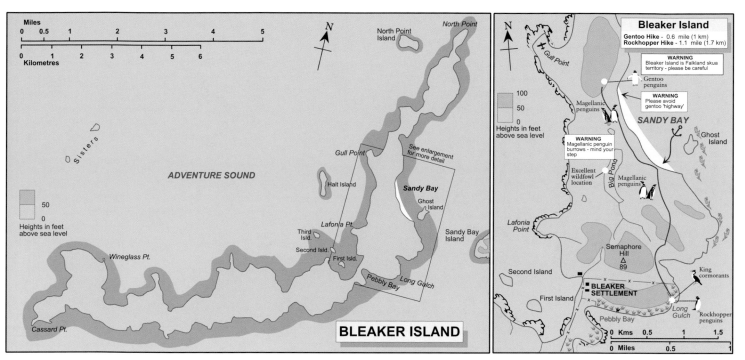

From 1990 until 1999 Bleaker Island belonged to Falkland Landholdings Limited and previously to the Falkland Islands Company, who in their turn, owned all Lafonia. Between about 1908 and the mid-1920's, the locally well-known agriculturist and amateur naturalist, Arthur Cobb, lived on the island. He was responsible for creating the extensive "greens" around the island that provide superb feeding grounds for sheep and cattle. In the days of high

POINTERS

▸ The northern end of Sandy Bay is particularly vulnerable to disturbance with penguins traversing back and forth to the colony on Penguin Hill.

▸ Watch out for Falkland skua attacks at the northern end of Sandy Bay and near the gentoo colony.

▸ Please do not disturb nesting gulls and oystercatchers on Sandy Bay beach.

Dog or white orchid

Ruddy-headed goose; most of the world's population can be found in the Falklands

wool prices the good quality pastures of Bleaker Island were exploited for breeding lambs to stock mainland farms. Today, the reduced number of just over 1,000 sheep complements organic meat production. Bleaker Island has been a sheep farm for many years, but under its new ownership is now shifting its emphasis from sheep to tourism. In 1970 the area to the north of the settlement was given statutory protection as a Wild Animal Sanctuary.

The settlement is situated in the centre of the Island where the sole permanent inhabitants, a farming couple, reside in the 60 year-old traditional house. Two other houses were constructed in 2000, the first for use as a self-catering cottage for tourists and the second for the owners. All the traditional camp facilities can be found including a shearing shed, a dairy, chicken runs, an electrical supply (with battery bank and wind generator giving 24-hour power), a water supply and vegetable gardens. A good grass airstrip 15 minutes drive from the settlement allows the Islander aircraft to land regularly, delivering passengers, mail and freight.

LANDING
Cruise ship passengers usually land by Zodiac in Sandy Bay. This 1 mile (1·6 km) long sand beach is fairly exposed due to the overall flatness of Bleaker Island, but its north/south orientation provides shelter from the prevailing westerly winds.

VEGETATION
The predominant vegetation of the Island consists of dwarf shrub heath and greens. If you are lucky you may see the yellow orchid, the attractive dog orchid and the beautiful red and yellow calceolaria, known as the lady's slipper. The yellow orchid is protected by law in the Falkland Islands and picking these orchids can incur a fine of up to £3,000 ($4,500).

HIKE & WILDLIFE
An easy short hike from Sandy Bay to Long Gulch (perhaps via Big Pond) will reward the walker with good views of many Falkland breeding birds. Watch out in particular for Magellanic penguins, crested and striated caracaras, Falkland skuas and the rare ruddy-

headed geese. Although fairly plentiful in the Falklands this goose has declined seriously in Patagonia and Tierra del Fuego. Snowy sheathbills can be seen regularly in summer, particularly around colonies of penguins or king cormorants, but they do not breed in the Falkland Islands. Many smaller birds may also be seen including the tussacbird, dark-faced ground-tyrant, and Magellanic snipe.

The northern end of Sandy Bay teems with gentoo penguins throughout the year, with approximately 1,300 breeding pairs on nearby Penguin Hill. One of the Island's principal features, the imaginatively named Big Pond, lies between Sandy Bay and the settlement, close to the island's highest point, Semaphore Hill 89 ft (27 m). This and the two smaller ponds just to the north are a popular habitat for Chiloë wigeon, silvery and white-tufted grebes and speckled and silver teal. It is also worth looking carefully for the flying steamer duck, a rare Falkland resident, which sometimes frequents Big Pond. Black-necked swans may also be seen here and a white-winged coot stayed here for several months during the summer of 1999. At least 37 species of birds are known to breed on the Island.

Although the settlement faces sheltered inshore waters to the west, the most scenic wildlife spot is just a short distance away over the rise towards the east coast. Here, among the tussac plantations, is a deep fissure in the cliffs known as Long Gulch, where a large number of rock cormorants nest. There are 750 pairs of rockhopper penguins breeding on the rocky ledges to the south of this gulch and more than 9,000 pairs of king cormorants breed in large groups on the nearby tussac fringes.

GEOLOGY

This low-lying island is formed of sandstone and mudstone that was originally deposited in a very large, deep lake about 250 million years ago. Tree trunks and other plant debris that floated into the lake have been preserved as fossils. Examples have been found on Semaphore Hill, close to the settlement.

Yellow orchid flower and plant – protected by law in the Falklands

Long Gulch – home to many rock cormorants

CARCASS ISLAND

FEATURES

▸ Striated caracara
▸ Gentoo and Magellanic penguins
▸ Peale's and Commerson's dolphins
▸ Carcass settlement and gardens
▸ Leopard Beach and Dyke Bay
▸ Abundant small birds including Cobb's wren which cannot survive on rat-infested islands
▸ Generally very tame birds
▸ Good example of tussac grass within Dyke Paddock

Commerson's dolphins

INTRODUCTION

Carcass Island lies to the north-west of the Falkland Islands archipelago and takes its name from HMS *Carcass* which visited in the late 18th century. It was first leased in 1872 by a legendary Danish seaman and sealer named Charles Hansen and is 4,680 acres (1,894 ha). He established Carcass Island as a sheep farm, building the settlement and fencing areas for livestock. Following the example of Arthur Felton on nearby West Point Island, the Hansens planted large areas of tussac for use as controlled winter animal grazing areas. In this aspect, they were conservationists long ahead of their time in the Falkland Islands, as were Cecil and Kitty Bertrand, the succeeding owners. A mature tussac plantation today covers much of the lower ground below Jason Hill to the east. The availability of abundant cover, and the absence of cats, rats and mice throughout the Island's history, has made for a spectacularly large population of small birds, which is now one of Carcass Island's most delightful features.

Present day owners, Rob and Lorraine McGill, who have lived on the Island for 27 years, continue the conservationist traditions. Rob lives here most of the year, and apart from a break during the winter, only travels infrequently to Stanley. Carcass Island has a grass airstrip 3 miles (4.8 km) north west of the settlement, where Rob meets the aircraft nearly

South American tern – impressive colony at Gothic Point

every day during the summer and once or twice a week in the winter. Although Carcass Island still supports around 900 sheep, tourism makes up much of its income. Rob and Lorraine utilise a freshwater spring in the valley behind the settlement for their water. Unlike much of the Falkland Islands, Carcass Island is water-rich and has 18 other water sources. Electrical power is available 24 hours a day from a generator, though this is rarely in use for more than 18 hours. The traditional fuel, peat, has been replaced recently by the more

CARCASS ISLAND: 51°18'S 60°34'W   **Ownership: Rob and Lorraine McGill**   **Size: 4,680 acres (1,894 ha)**   **Population: 2 to 4 in summer**

Leopard Beach, Carcass Island

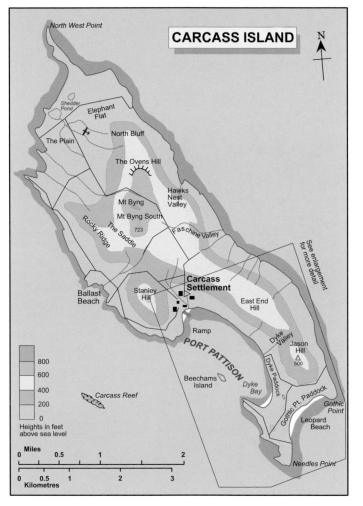

CARCASS ISLAND

N

North West Point

Shedder Pond

Elephant Flat

The Plain

North Bluff

The Ovens Hill

Hawks Nest Valley

Mt Byng

Mt Byng South

723

The Saddle

Faschine Valley

Rocky Ridge

Ballast Beach

Stanley Hill

Carcass Settlement

East End Hill

Ramp

Dyke Valley

PORT PATTISON

Beechams Island

Dyke Bay

Jason Hill
△ 500

Dyke Paddock

Gothic Pt. Paddock

Gothic Point

Leopard Beach

Carcass Reef

Needles Point

See enlargement for more detail

800
600
400
200
0
Heights in feet above sea level

Miles
0   0.5   1   2

0   0.5   1   2   3
Kilometres

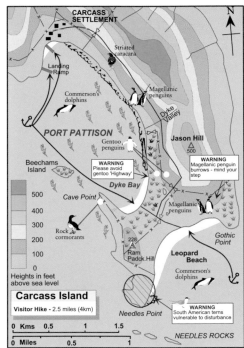

CARCASS SETTLEMENT

N

Landing Ramp

Striated caracara

Commerson's dolphins

Magellanic penguins

Dyke Valley

PORT PATTISON

Gentoo penguins

Jason Hill
△ 500

Beechams Island

Cave Point

WARNING
Please avoid gentoo 'Highway'

Dyke Bay

WARNING
Magellanic penguin burrows - mind your step

Rock cormorants

Magellanic penguins

228
△ Ram Padock Hill

Gothic Point

Leopard Beach

Commerson's dolphins

500
400
300
200
100
0
Heights in feet above sea level

Carcass Island

Visitor Hike - 2.5 miles (4km)

Needles Point

WARNING
South American terns vulnerable to disturbance

NEEDLES ROCKS

0   Kms   0.5   1   1.5

0   Miles   0.5   1

POINTERS

▸ Avoid the large areas of kelp beds in Dyke Bay when travelling in Zodiacs.

▸ Take care not to disturb the South American tern colony on Gothic Point.

▸ Take care walking through tussac near the shoreline as it sometimes hides steep rocks and cliffs and it is easy to lose your footing.

The settlement and its gardens

convenient oil and gas which is delivered by the local vessel MV *Tamar FI*. There are plans for wind power in the future.

The settlement gardens contain a colourful array of flowers, Monterey cypress trees planted in the 1930's, and a variety of shrubs including New Zealand cabbage palms and New Zealand flax. Carcass Island is self-sufficient in organic vegetables, meat and dairy products and there are a number of laying hens. Despite this abundance, eggs are still required from other parts of the Islands in order to provide cakes for hungry cruise ship visitors.

LANDINGS

There are three possible landing sites on Carcass Island, the choice of which will be determined by each individual vessel in the light of conditions prevailing at the time. On all Zodiac routes there is a good chance to spot Commerson's and Peale's dolphins.

The landing sites to the east of the settlement, Dyke Bay and Leopard Beach, are on impressive stretches of fine white sand. Leopard Beach is 1,090 yds (1 km) long and has a high wall of sand dunes which provide shelter. Dyke Bay in Port Pattison has a backing of tussac stands. From both beach landings a 2 mile (3·1 km) nature trail leads to the settlement.

For those not wishing to undertake the nature trail, landings can often be made in Port Pattison near to the settlement, which is also where the walking parties will usually be picked up. Settlement landings are on to a small sand and rocky beach or alternatively use the recently constructed wooden landing ramp 300 yds (275 m) south-east of the settlement. This allows a dry landing and has stainless steel netting to prevent slipping.

When landing at Leopard Beach, the ship will pass the Needles Rocks just off the southern tip of Carcass Island. Cannon balls have been found here, a reminder that ships used these rocks as target practice in past centuries. Immediately on rounding the Needles, a huge colony of South American terns may be seen. These attractive birds, which nest here irregularly, are particularly vulnerable to disturbance. Please take care to avoid this area until after incubation (October to January).

Sea cabbage – found on sandy beaches but, despite its name and soft woolly appearance, is slimy to eat

Black-chinned siskin (above) and Black-throated finch (below) – just two of the small birds that breed in the dense tussac within Dyke Paddock

HIKE – WILDLIFE – VEGETATION

At all landing sites a prolific number of shore birds are to be seen, including the endemic Falkland flightless steamer duck. From mid September through January they often have a brood of chicks following their every move, so take care not to disturb them. At Dyke Bay beach, particularly, you will be greeted by the endearing tussacbirds, which will dare to come closer and closer until they are practically standing on your boots. Magellanic penguin burrows are littered between the two landing beaches (in Gothic and Dyke Bay paddocks and along the rocky shoreline) so mind your step. Falkland skua chicks can sometimes be observed trying to hide in the low vegetation, their anxious parents soaring ahead. Keep an eye out for any aggressive behaviour from these birds (particularly in November through to January, their chick-rearing time). Upland geese are also abundant in this area; they mate for life and each pair has its own closely guarded territory. The dense tussac area within Dyke Paddock provides breeding habitat for small birds such as the Cobb's wren (an endemic), black-throated finch, grass wren, Magellanic snipe, tussacbird and Falkland thrush.

The unmarked nature trail follows the fence line from Gothic Paddock up to a small gate on Jason Hill and then takes a westerly direction towards the two main gentoo colonies nestling under Jason Hill. This hike has a climb of 492 ft (150 m) and the terrain is easy going with lush green grass interspersed with diddle-dee, berry-lobelia, balsam bog and introduced sheep's sorrel. The vegetation is varied, with several low-growing cushion or carpet-forming plants. Sea cabbage (which has a soft woolly surface but despite its name, is slimy to eat) is found on the sand beaches, tall rush and tussac grass in paddocks, pig vine, the widespread resinous shrub diddle-dee and some eye catching patches of European gorse near the settlement. Gorse has a beautiful, coconut-scented yellow flower in October and November and was introduced to the Islands by 19th century settlers who planted it as hedges to manage livestock and to provide shelter for gardens.

Carcass Island has large breeding colonies of Magellanic penguins and gentoo penguins (610 pairs). Magellanic penguins are often found burrowing under tussac pedestals. However, since the decrease of tussac, they are increasingly found burrowing in coastal heathland. During the walk, please be careful not to crush their underground homes built in the soft peaty soil. They are so abundant on this island they even nest under Rob's house. Upon leaving the gentoo colonies, the trail heads

44

Magellanic penguin – abundant on Carcass, even nesting under the owner's house

Berry-lobelia

across Dyke Valley toward the shoreline and on to the settlement where you will have the chance to sample a traditional Falklands tea. The terrain provides easy walking, mostly down hill to the settlement. On the way, coastal birds such as blackish oystercatchers, black-crowned night-herons and rock cormorants can be seen along the rocky shoreline. Striated caracaras swoop majestically along this coastline. Carcass Island has 14 breeding pairs of this rare species. In the 2000-01 season, a single nestling in a nest on the Port Pattison coast was nurtured by three adults, acting cooperatively as if they were a pair. Although remarkably tame for a large bird of prey, some pairs are very aggressive during the breeding season, particularly when they have chicks in the nest. You could be attacked if you approach too closely, especially between late October and January.

GEOLOGY

The island is dominated by Mount Byng 700 ft (214 m) and other lesser peaks which undulate along its length. Most of this island is made up of hard, white quartzite deposited at the margin of a shallow sea about 400 million years ago. The originally horizontal layers of rock have been folded in such a way that slightly older and softer, yellowish-brown sandstone can be seen in the vicinity of the settlement and main beach. Dark grey flecks and streaks in this brown sandstone are all that remain of primitive plants that were washed out to sea.

Rob McGill

The view across Port Pattison

GEORGE AND BARREN ISLANDS

Cobb's wren

FEATURES

- Elephant seal and southern sea lion colonies
- Tiny and Emily Islands
- Superb bird life
- Tea and a chat with the May family
- Opportunity to watch sheep shearing
- Abundant southern giant petrel colonies
- Gentoo and Magellanic penguins
- No cats, rats or mice

These intriguing islands, located to the south-west of East Falkland, were not previously opened for tourists. For a century and a half they belonged to the Falkland Islands Company and were used for sheep farming. In 2001, both islands were bought by the May family, living on George Island throughout the summer months. There is good, sheltered anchorage and Zodiac landings on to rocky shores but it is not advisable to use either of the jetties, as they are unsafe. There are plans to build landing ramps in the future.

Because both islands are free of rodents they are home to a truly brilliant range of wildlife. They each support more than 30 species of birds including the tussacbird, Cobb's wren, southern giant petrel and ruddy-headed goose. Walking is easy with the highest points, Peat Bog Hill on George Island and Tea Point Ridge on Barren Island, being only 60 ft (15 m) above sea level.

GEORGE ISLAND

Within a fairly short walk of the settlement there is a large colony of southern sea lions on the western shore. Take care, because much of the island is riddled with Magellanic penguin burrows. Along the shore there are several breeding colonies of the magnificent southern giant petrels and sooty shearwaters have been found breeding in burrows on Strike Off Point.

Nearby there are some interesting peat mounds on an eroded stretch of the shore, which contain large amounts of seal bones. There is a theory that this was a belt of tussac grass burnt out by early sealers in order to catch these poor creatures. These peat mounds can also be seen on Barren Island.

BARREN ISLAND

The waters around the jetty on Barren Island have been silted up with peat dust from erosion. However it is possible to land close to the old settlement and at Tea Point. Barren has a large colony of gentoo penguins (1,300 breeding pairs), elephant seals, southern sea lions and southern giant petrels and a vast array of other bird life, including striated caracara and Cobb's wren.

TINY AND EMILY ISLANDS

These two small tussac islands just north of Barren Island are teeming with elephant seals and southern sea lions. The May family welcomes visitors to these fantastic islands, having time for a friendly chat and an offer of tea in their home. They will also provide the opportunity to watch sheep shearing. Chris and Lindsey May can be contacted on VHF channel 16.

Close encounter with a male elephant seal

GEORGE & BARREN ISLANDS: 52°21'S 59°45'W   Ownership: Chris and Lindsey May   Size: 8,772 acres (3,550 ha)   Population: 2

1,300 breeding pairs of gentoo penguin can be found on Barren Island

GYPSY COVE

FEATURES

- Magellanic penguins
- Black-crowned night herons nesting on the cliffs
- Expansive scenic views of beach and dune
- Black-throated finches
- Red-backed hawks

WWII Vickers gun at Gypsy Cove

INTRODUCTION

Gypsy Cove lies less than 4 miles (6 km) from Stanley, to the north-west of Yorke Bay. This secluded crescent of white sand is well protected from the prevailing winds. The area belongs to the Falkland Islands Government.

Yorke Bay and parts of Gypsy Cove are fenced off to prevent access to minefields. These areas must not be entered in any circumstances.

Among the prominent features of this area are the desolate remains of World War II guns used in the defence of the outer harbour, Port William, over which turkey vultures can often be seen describing lazy circles in the sky. This was one of about 14 outposts which ringed Stanley manned by men of the Falkland Islands Defence Force.

HIKE AND WILDLIFE

The main features at Gypsy Cove are sign posted by Falklands Conservation and the gravel path provides a superb view of Yorke Bay. This picturesque sandy bay is a favoured feeding ground of waders, waterfowl and gulls. Birds seen frequently include Magellanic and blackish oystercatchers, two-banded plovers, kelp geese, Falkland steamer ducks, Patagonian crested ducks, rock cormorants, dolphin gulls and kelp gulls.

Gypsy Cove has a breeding population of about 320 pairs of Magellanic penguins (1999). The beach itself is backed by penguin burrows amid patches of tussac grass, cinnamon grass, dry heath and dune, which are home to the Falkland thrush, dark-faced ground-tyrant, grass wren and the striking black-throated finch which is an endemic sub-species and remarkably tame at this site. Out to sea, South American terns, which nest on the offshore islet, can be seen with Falkland skuas, Magellanic and gentoo penguins. The Cove is also frequented by the occasional sea lion hoping to catch penguins and fish.

Further north towards Ordnance Point, the low cliffs provide nesting sites for rock cormorants and black-crowned night herons. The waters around this coastline offer an opportunity for spotting

Woolly ragwort – a Falklands endemic

GYPSY COVE: 51°41'S 57°48'W   Ownership: F.I. Government Reserve   Size: about 20 acres (8 ha)   Population: 0

Peregrine falcons perch on the cliff edge looking for suitable prey

POINTERS

▸ Do not enter the mined areas.

▸ Sensible footwear is needed for the gravel path and walking around the coastline.

▸ Stay clear of the beach as this can prevent penguins returning to feed their chicks.

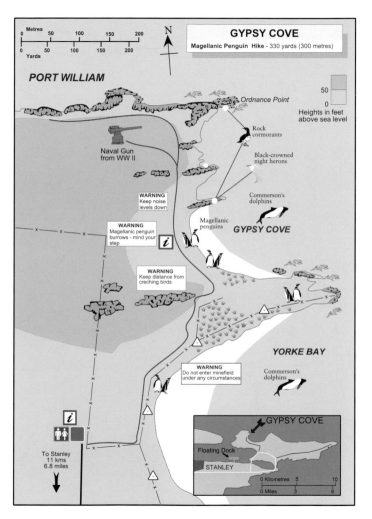

GYPSY COVE

Magellanic Penguin Hike - 330 yards (300 metres)

PORT WILLIAM

Ordnance Point

Rock cormorants

Black-crowned night herons

Naval Gun from WW II

Heights in feet above sea level

Commerson's dolphins

WARNING
Keep noise levels down

WARNING
Magellanic penguin burrows - mind your step

Magellanic penguins

GYPSY COVE

WARNING
Keep distance from creching birds

YORKE BAY

WARNING
Do not enter minefield under any circumstances

Commerson's dolphins

To Stanley
11 kms
6.8 miles

GYPSY COVE

Floating Dock

STANLEY

seabirds such as sooty shearwaters, southern giant petrels, king and rock cormorants. Ordnance Point provides a good vantage point to take photographs of the Cove and the surrounding coastline. It also features an area of balsam-bog, a typical Falkland plant of exposed windy areas. The occasional red-backed hawk can be seen foraging around for small birds. Watch out also for a peregrine falcon perched on the sea cliffs waiting for suitable prey.

VEGETATION

Most of the site is covered by dwarf shrub heath dominated by diddle-dee and has plenty of wild flowers, including the pale maiden, the fragrant vanilla daisy and the endemic woolly ragwort. Near the beach there are areas of gorse which are swathed in bright yellow flowers from spring to summer. Look out for the large white or pink flower of scurvygrass (a native *Oxalis*), so named because the sharp-tasting leaves have a high vitamin C content and were once collected and eaten by sailors to prevent scurvy. Traditionally a non-alcoholic drink called scurvy wine was made from this flower.

Magellanic (left) and blackish oystercatchers (right) can both be found at Gypsy Cove. Blackish oystercatchers have a preference for rocky shores while the Magellanic prefers sandy beaches backed by grassy slopes. Often the two species are to be found side by side

KIDNEY COVE

FEATURES

- Four species of penguin (gentoo, king, rockhopper and Magellanic)
- Red-backed hawks, peregrine falcons, turkey vultures
- Wonderful scenery and superb views of Stanley

INTRODUCTION

Kidney Cove is partly owned by Adrian and Lisa Lowe of the Murrell Farm which covers 10,000 acres (4,047 ha). It is principally a sheep farm, with some horses and cattle. The settlement is 9 miles (14·5 km) west of Kidney Cove. The family undertake the one hour overland trip into Stanley for stores every few weeks and must wait for low tides before they can cross the Murrell River.

Kidney Cove and the nearby Kidney Island (both names reflect the shape of the coastline) to the north of Port William, are just 7 miles (10 km) from Stanley. Sparrow Cove, to the south-west, provides a sheltered natural harbour for access to Kidney Cove.

LANDING

The only access by sea is a dry landing using the floating pontoon to the south-west of Sparrow Cove. The rocky shoreline supports an abundant population of birds including species such as Falkland flightless steamer ducks, Patagonian crested ducks, upland geese, blackish oystercatchers and the occasional brown-hooded gull.

Sparrow Cove was the final resting place in the Falkland Islands for the SS *Great Britain*. This vessel, built in 1843 by I K Brunel, was of a revolutionary design being the first propeller driven iron ship. She was used as a breakwater in Sparrow Cove and in 1970 was transported back to

Upland geese frequent the shoreline

Britain where she is being restored and preserved at Bristol docks.

Visitors are met by the owners and local guides and are taken by Land Rover to the gentoo colonies, a journey of approximately half an hour. This is an experience in itself, as overland trips are an essential part of many Islanders' lifestyle, given that road systems are fairly limited. From ship back to ship the trip takes two hours.

The overland journey follows the rocky coastline of Sparrow Cove, passing a dam on the north side. This dam, constructed in 1921, was used to provide fresh water for ships. Passing through a wire gate the Land Rovers follow the fence line up a steep climb of 350 ft (106 m) along the eastern side of Mount Low. A panoramic photograph of Stanley and the surrounding hills is a must from this vantage point and also the stunning views of Kidney Cove.

Falkland skuas patrol the penguin colonies

KIDNEY COVE: 51°38'S 57°46'W   **Ownership: Adrian and Lisa Lowe**   **Size: about 10,000 acres (4,047 ha)**   **Population: 6**

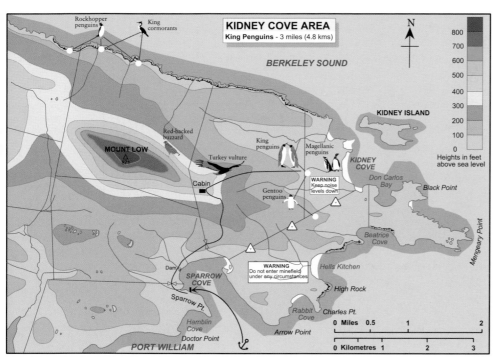

KIDNEY COVE AREA
King Penguins - 3 miles (4.8 kms)

N

Rockhopper penguins

King cormorants

BERKELEY SOUND

KIDNEY ISLAND

Red-backed buzzard

MOUNT LOW
△
874

Turkey vulture

King penguins

Magellanic penguins

KIDNEY COVE

Cabin

Don Carlos Bay

Black Point

Gentoo penguins

WARNING
Keep noise levels down

△

Beatrice Cove

△

Mengeary Point

Dam

SPARROW COVE

WARNING
Do not enter minefield under any circumstances

Hells Kitchen

△

High Rock

Sparrow Pt.

Rabbit Cove

Charles Pt.

Hamblin Cove

Arrow Point

Doctor Point

PORT WILLIAM

800
700
600
500
400
300
200
100
0
Heights in feet above sea level

0 Miles 0.5 1 2

0 Kilometres 1 2 3

WILDLIFE

Nestling to the east of Mount Low is a cabin used by land-based tourists. The Murrell Farm has four breeding species of penguin - king, rockhopper, gentoo and Magellanic. Kidney Cove contains one of very few breeding colonies of king penguins in the Falkland Islands as well as gentoo and Magellanic penguins. The rockies are a little further afield and you may get the opportunity to see them as a land-based visitor. The Land Rovers then head east to the several sub colonies of gentoo penguins, the locations of which are likely to vary widely from year to year.

Turkey vultures scavenge around the penguin colonies

53

Kidney Cove has four species of penguin breeding, from top to bottom king, Magellanic, gentoo and rockhopper

These colonies (comprising 1,625 breeding pairs) are typically within 110 yds (100 m) of each other and walking between the colonies is easy. King penguins are found between the gentoo colonies. Although currently in low numbers, the population of kings is thought to be increasing. Albino gentoo are occasionally found in the Falkland Islands and one was sighted here in 2000.

Nesting Falkland skuas have a fearsome reputation when protecting their nests and territories. Local practice is to carry a small stick above your head for protection. Skuas have been known to knock a dog completely off its feet and people off horses when they feel their territory is being threatened.

Turkey vultures are the largest and most common bird of prey in the Islands. They can be seen in great numbers on the eastern coastline of this area feeding on dead penguins, chicks, and sheep, thereby helping to keep camps clean. Occasionally, red-backed hawks can be seen in the rocky areas of Mount Low. Introduced brown hares breed in abundance further to the east of the area occasionally straying near the gentoo colonies. These have been in the Islands since the 19th century and have become widespread and common in parts of East Falkland.

GEOLOGY

This small, attractive cove is surrounded by hard, pale grey quartzite. The beds of rock originated as layers of sand deposited about 400 million years

The rockhopper colony at Kidney Cove

ago beneath the shallow water at the margin of a large sea. Through time, the once-horizontal rock beds have been folded and tilted so that many are now steeply inclined.

The hard quartzite also gives rise to another famous Falklands phenomenon – stone runs. These river-like accumulations of large boulders were formed during the last ice age, between 14,000 and 25,000 years ago. Recent studies hint that they may be 60,000 years old. Although the Falkland Islands were not covered by glaciers, they were subjected to a severe tundra-type climate. Intense frost action broke up the quartzite layers into boulders which, as they slowly slipped downhill, were heaved and sorted by countless cycles of freezing and thawing into stripes and boulder fields.

Kidney Island from Mount Low

NEW ISLAND

FEATURES

▸ 41 species of breeding birds including king penguins (New Island North Nature Reserve)
▸ Large population of breeding thin-billed prions
▸ Several colonies of black-browed albatross
▸ Fur seal colonies
▸ Historical buildings including whaling station remains
▸ Dramatic scenery
▸ Breeding groups of Peale's dolphin
▸ Enough sites of interest to fill an entire day

Sooty shearwater

HISTORY AND INTRODUCTION

New Island, which is the most remote of all the inhabited islands, is situated in the extreme west of the Falklands and contains some of the finest scenery and largest concentrations of wildlife to be found in the archipelago. It has been a popular destination for smaller expedition cruise vessels since the early 1970's.

From as early as 1774 and for half a century onwards, New Island provided a refuge and often a winter home for North American whaling ships. Coffin Island, Coffin Harbour and Barnard Passage today bear the names of well-known whaling and sealing captains from that era. Coffin Island is now a nature reserve owned and managed by Falklands Conservation, as are six other smaller islands clustered around the main island.

In August 1860 the first Crown lease for the Island was issued and the sale of 160 acres (65 ha) marked the first recorded 'settlement'. Livestock was introduced at this time and sheep farming for wool became the mainstay of the Island's economy for over a century.

In 1979 New Island was divided into two equally sized and independently run properties. Both of these are run today as nature reserves and all inhabitants live in the attractive, brightly-coloured settlement on the southern section of New Island overlooking Coffin Harbour.

Comprised largely of hard quartz sandstone more than 400 million years old, the Island's strata are tilted in such a way that the land sweeps up dramatically from the sheltered eastern seaboard of beautiful sandy bays and natural harbours to towering sea cliffs on the west. These cliffs are exposed to the prevailing winds and are often pounded by high seas. New Island is one of the driest places in the Falkland Islands with rainfall amounting annually to less than 16 inches (40 cms).

New Island North Nature Reserve
Ownership: Tony and Kim Chater
Size: 1,181 ha (2,920 acres)

New Island South Wildlife Reserve
**Ownership: New Island South Conservation Trust,
      founder Ian J. Strange**
Size: 1,181 ha (2,920 acres)

NEW ISLAND: 51°43'S 61°18'W   **Size: 5,840 acres (2,363 ha)**   **Population: 3 (New Island North); 1 (New Island South)**

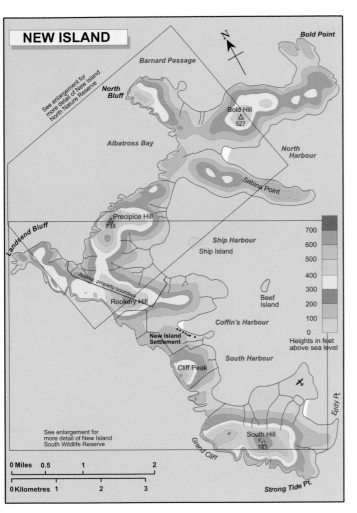

NEW ISLAND

Bold Point

Barnard Passage

North Bluff

See enlargement for more detail of New Island North Nature Reserve

Bold Hill
△ 527

Albatross Bay

North Harbour

Sabina Point

Landsend Bluff

Precipice Hill
△ 735

Ship Harbour

Ship Island

Approx. property boundary

Rookery Hill

Beef Island

Coffin's Harbour

| 700 |
| 600 |
| 500 |
| 400 |
| 300 |
| 200 |
| 100 |
| 0 |

Heights in feet above sea level

New Island Settlement

South Harbour

Cliff Peak

Eddy Pt.

See enlargement for more detail of New Island South Wildlife Reserve

South Hill
△ 743

Grand Cliff

0 Miles   0.5   1   2

0 Kilometres   1   2   3

Strong Tide Pt.

Red-backed hawks can be found all over the island

POINTERS

▸ No smoking is permitted anywhere on the island.

▸ Fur seals are susceptible to disturbance. Move slowly and keep quiet when near colonies.

▸ The gentoo penguins are more wary in the Falklands than in the Antarctic due to the presence of more predators and, in particular, southern sea lions. Please take extra care around the colonies.

▸ If possible avoid areas where prions are breeding; burrows are shallow in sandy/peaty soil and very fragile.

New Island North Nature Reserve

Tony Chater

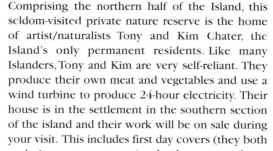

The yellow violet has benefitted from the tussac restoration on New Island

Comprising the northern half of the Island, this seldom-visited private nature reserve is the home of artist/naturalists Tony and Kim Chater, the Island's only permanent residents. Like many Islanders, Tony and Kim are very self-reliant. They produce their own meat and vegetables and use a wind turbine to produce 24-hour electricity. Their house is in the settlement in the southern section of the island and their work will be on sale during your visit. This includes first day covers (they both design postage stamps), calendars, postcards, art work and Tony's well-known book "The Falklands".

Of the 61 bird species that are known to breed regularly in the archipelago, 41 do so here, including four of the five Falkland penguins. Two species of seal are also resident; the South American fur seal and the southern sea lion, and there are several breeding groups of Peale's dolphins in the inshore waters.

Since the removal of the livestock from the reserve in 1987, with the exception of 50 sheep kept in one area as a domestic meat supply, there has been a rapid expansion of the tussac grass areas and a corresponding increase in the number and variety of flowering plants. Lady's slipper, yellow violet and pale maidens are found in profusion, while the rare yellow orchid is also present.

In a further effort to return the property to its natural state, the Chaters have made extensive and successful efforts to re-establish native tussac grass by hand-planting approximately half a million plants.

Fur Seal Colonies

From a sand-beach landing in Ship Harbour, the walk to this most accessible of the Falkland's fur seal colonies covers a total return distance of about 3 miles (4·8 km) and involves a gentle climb of 300 ft (92 m). In all, this is a very good leg stretch and should only be undertaken by the fitter tourists.

The landing site is rich in Magellanic penguins, speckled teal, ruddy-headed geese, steamer ducks, long-tailed meadowlarks and Magellanic oystercatchers. The walk proceeds up a beautiful and gently inclining valley peppered with literally thousands of thin-billed prion holes. Please stay on the track and be especially vigilant not to trample on these delicate nesting burrows which may contain birds, chicks or eggs.

Once at the top of the rise there is a fine view of the headland called Landsend Bluff and tucked away at the bottom of cliffs, are the fur seal. On a quiet day you can hear them from some distance away. As you get closer please remember that these animals are very easily disturbed. For their benefit and your own, keep the noise down and move slowly.

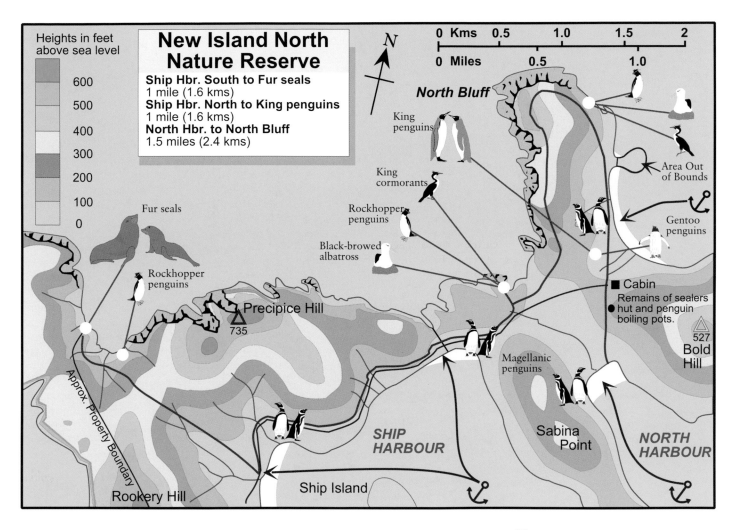

New Island North Nature Reserve

Heights in feet above sea level

600
500
400
300
200
100
0

Ship Hbr. South to Fur seals
1 mile (1.6 kms)
Ship Hbr. North to King penguins
1 mile (1.6 kms)
North Hbr. to North Bluff
1.5 miles (2.4 kms)

N

0 Kms 0.5 1.0 1.5 2

0 Miles 0.5 1.0

North Bluff

King penguins

King cormorants

Rockhopper penguins

Black-browed albatross

Area Out of Bounds

Gentoo penguins

■ Cabin
● Remains of sealers hut and penguin boiling pots.

527
Bold Hill

Fur seals

Rockhopper penguins

△ Precipice Hill
735

Magellanic penguins

SHIP HARBOUR

Sabina Point

NORTH HARBOUR

Approx. Property Boundary

Rookery Hill

Ship Island

59

Both crested (above) and striated caracaras ('johnny rooks') can be seen on New Island

This is a breeding area and there are young pups often hidden from view. Keep your profile from appearing along the skyline and you will be rewarded by a much better look at the animals behaving naturally. Close by is a very attractive rockhopper penguin rookery.

The route away leads in a south-southeasterly direction by way of the west side of Rookery Hill and takes you across the property boundary into the southern section of New Island. It is slightly longer than the first part of the walk and ends at the settlement rookery from where you can return to your ship. Four hours should be allowed for this excursion.

The North End

The area known as the 'North End' is one of sweeping green valleys, open sandy beaches, magnificent cliffs and seascapes. In a relatively small area you are able to see a variety and profusion of Falkland wildlife unsurpassed elsewhere in the archipelago. Flocks of upland and ruddy-headed geese graze everywhere. The gentoo colony includes over 6,000 breeding pairs and is the largest of its type in the world. Sea lions regularly hunt and kill penguins along the shore. Dating back to sealing times in the early 19th century, there are the remains of an old stone shelter and two stone rings where thousands of penguins were boiled and rendered down for their oil in large iron pots. Two pairs of king penguin have bred regularly for the last twelve years and up

to nine individuals can sometimes be seen. 5,000 Magellanic penguins gather each autumn in close-knit bunches for their annual moult. Some 5,000 pairs of black-browed albatross nest at one site alone. Together with king cormorants and rockhopper penguins they form an impressive assemblage, set amongst rich green grass, tussac and bright orange-lichen rocks. This is one of the most colourful and photogenic of all Falkland seabird colonies. Huge numbers of thin-billed prions create a nocturnal cacophony in the spring and early summer. Over 200 pairs of Falkland skua are resident from October to April feeding on the prions by day and night. All five of the Islands' birds of prey breed here, including a large number of the striated caracara or 'johnny rook', one of the rarest, tamest, and most inquisitive birds of prey in the world. Throughout the summer these avian rascals vie for supremacy with the powerful skuas that hold breeding territories all around the seabird colonies.

The whole of this wonderful area can be approached from any one of three anchorages. The distances vary, as indicated on the map, but in each case the walks are over fairly easy and dry ground. It can also be possible for passengers to be dropped off at one location and picked up at another, incorporating a walk of up to 3 miles (4·8 km).

Overleaf : Black-browed albatross and chick (left); Gentoo penguin colony at the North End (right) and gentoos coming ashore (inset)

The imposing scenery of the North End

New Island South Wildlife Reserve

Ian J. Strange

Owner: New Island South Conservation Trust. Registered Public Charity. UK Charity Commission No 1047676. Trust Founder Ian J. Strange, naturalist, author and artist continues to run the reserve.

New Island South's western coast with view to Landsend Bluff

New Island Settlement colony of rockhopper penguin, king cormorant and black-browed albatross

The Trust ensures that the southern half of New Island will remain a protected wildlife reserve in perpetuity by law. A conservation project established by the founder in 1971 is therefore assured for the future. Learn more of the Trust's aims and work by visiting the "Geoffrey C Hughes Field Station" situated in the settlement. Visitors and those passing through are welcome to New Island South, but for your guidance we advise that the settlement and airstrip are situated on New Island South property.

For ship borne visitors landing at the small sheltered sand beach below the settlement, an old stone building at the beachhead is a further reminder of the island's history and connections with North America. A frequent visitor and possibly the earliest resident of New Island was Captain Charles H Barnard of the whaler *Nanina*. Barnard and four of his crew were marooned here from June 1813 until November 1814. They built a rough stone shelter, the origins of which now form the larger and partly restored building known as the Barnard Memorial Museum.

Settlement Colonies

One of the most attractive areas lies some ten minutes easy walk from the Barnard Memorial Museum. This walk takes you from the low-lying eastern side of the island, to the more exposed western side. The route lies over a grassy plain, a feeding and breeding area for large numbers of upland geese. Approaching the west side the scene changes, presenting formidable sea cliffs rising to over 550 ft (168 m) which form the Island's western coastline. The vegetation also changes on this side, with sea spray assisting the development of a lush growth of native Fuegian couch grass, wild celery, shore meadow-grass and tussac grass.

Approaching these cliffs, the relative quietness of the valley is interrupted with the raucous calls of birds. Black-browed albatross soar effortlessly on updrafts. Streams of king cormorants come and go through this air space. Falkland skuas, dolphin gulls, turkey vultures and striated caracaras add to the scene. Please pay attention to where you walk, as the route here can sometimes be slippery from sea spray. Several thousand pairs of nesting rockhopper penguins add to this impressive scene.

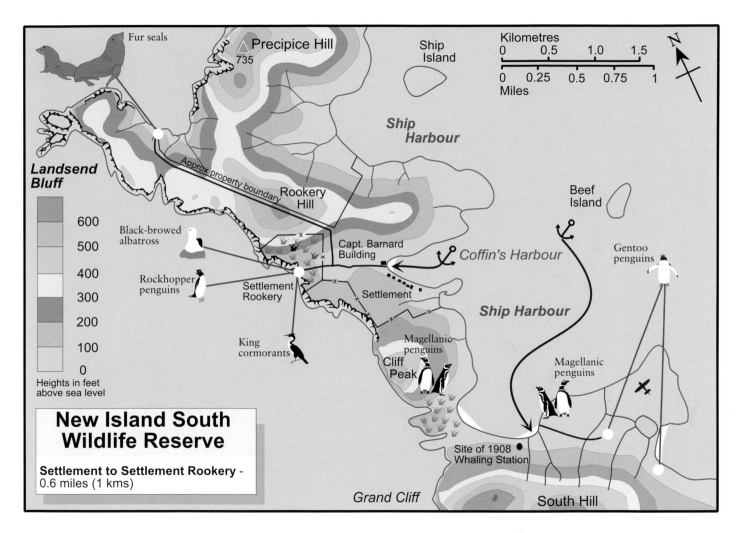

Fur seals

Precipice Hill
735

Ship Island

Ship Harbour

Kilometres
0   0.5   1.0   1.5

Miles
0   0.25   0.5   0.75   1

N

Landsend Bluff

Approx property boundary

Rookery Hill

Beef Island

600
500
400
300
200
100
0

Heights in feet
above sea level

Black-browed albatross

Rockhopper penguins

Settlement Rookery

King cormorants

Capt. Barnard Building

Coffin's Harbour

Settlement

Ship Harbour

Gentoo penguins

Magellanic penguins

Cliff Peak

Magellanic penguins

Magellanic penguins

Site of 1908 Whaling Station

Grand Cliff

South Hill

New Island South Wildlife Reserve

Settlement to Settlement Rookery -
0.6 miles (1 kms)

Scurvygrass

In tight breeding groups amongst the penguins are king cormorants and dispersed over the area are black-browed albatross, each bird sitting on its nest pedestal formed from mud and vegetation.

Take advantage of the scenery by bearing left round the edge of the penguin colony. From the higher ground one looks down into a natural amphitheatre, the sides lined with nesting penguins. From the same position one has a commanding view of New Island's towering cliffs. At the base of these watch out for large rafts of penguins landing through the surf and climbing traditional routes to the colonies.

New Island is particularly important as a breeding ground for the thin-billed prion. These seabirds come ashore only during darkness to take turns at incubation or to feed a chick in a nest chamber below ground. At these times the entire Island resounds to their calls. Many areas are pitted with their burrows and birds in nest chambers during the day will often be heard calling with a low murmuring sound in response to your footsteps. Be especially vigilant and skirt burrow areas, as the dry soil easily gives way and a nest could be destroyed. Please try to avoid marked areas denoting field research areas.

Fur Seal Colonies

Fur seal colonies are accessible in both the northern and southern properties. For visitors to

New Island settlement

Looking towards Beaver Island across the Settlement

New Island South the route is best commenced from the settlement on a general heading of north-northwest towards Rookery Hill. Please obtain advice before setting out as the route is not easy walking. The rewards are spectacular scenery and some of the best views of fur seal in the Falklands.

From the top of Rookery Hill, 600 ft (183 m), there is a fine view of the headland called

Fur seals bask on the rocks

Landsend Bluff to the north-northwest. Tucked away at the bottom of cliffs forming the bay to the right hand side of the Bluff, are the fur seal. On a quiet day you can clearly hear them from some distance. Please remember that these animals are very easily disturbed. Keep quiet, move slowly and you will be rewarded by a much better view of a breeding group with their pups. For your safety and to prevent disturbance, please avoid the two small but accessible colonies closer to the Landsend Bluff area.

Beef Island (left) and Coffin Island (right), Falklands Conservation Nature Reserves seen from New Island settlement

Whaling Station 1906-1916 and Gentoo Penguin Colonies

The remains of this whaling station lie in South Harbour. Not to be confused with the much earlier American whaling era, it was the first and only land-based whaling station in the Falkland Islands. It was initially planned by Alexander Lange in 1906. In 1908 Salvesen & Co of Leith took over and built a station employing some 80 men. Catches were small and in 1916 the station closed and moved to South Georgia. Today the site with its rusting winches, steam boilers and machinery offers a glance back into the history of this whaling industry. Take care when exploring, as remains lie partly hidden in the vegetation.

A short distance further south from the whaling station the visitor is presented with yet another vista. In contrast to the steep western scenery a flat open valley emerges dotted with colonies of gentoo penguins, large numbers of geese and Magellanic penguins.

Magellanic snipe, one of over 40 bird species breeding on New Island

67

PORT HOWARD

FEATURES

▶ Narrows Island
▶ Sheep shearing and dog handling
▶ 1982 Conflict Museum
▶ Explore the settlement and meet a small Falkland Islands community
▶ Refreshments and hospitality

Port Howard lies behind a rocky coastal ridge on the west coast of Falkland Sound. It is one of the last big farms of the Falkland Islands with 80 miles (128 km) of coastline and 40 miles (64 km) of boundary fencing surrounding its 200,000 acres (80,940 ha). Approximately 45,000 sheep and 500 cattle are ranched with 550 bales of prime wool being produced annually.

James Lovegrove Waldron, an English farmer looking for land to develop, first leased land at Port Howard in 1866. The property remained in Waldron hands until 1990 when it was sold to Robin and Rodney Lee, descendents of Jacob Lee, one of the farm's first shepherds. The farm now belongs to Port Howard Farming Ltd..

Adjacent to the entrance of the harbour is Narrows Island, never grazed by sheep or cattle and home to at least 63 species of plants, some endemic. Narrows Island can easily be reached by Zodiac, but visitors should watch out for the southern sea lions dozing in the tussac grass.

Landing at this picturesque settlement can be either on to a wooden jetty or on the rocky shoreline near the sheep shearing shed. A warm welcome will be given by the many Commerson's dolphins that frequent the water near Port Howard settlement. Shearing demonstrations can be given in the appropriate season. A gravel track, half a mile (750 m), leads to Port Howard Lodge and the heart of the settlement. In the grounds of the lodge is a small museum commemorating the events of 1982 when 1,000 Argentine troops occupied Port Howard. SAS Captain Gavin John Hamilton MC who died during this conflict is buried in the settlement cemetery.

A chance to meet the locals and to enjoy a traditional Falklands 'smoko' (tea and coffee with homemade baking) will be provided in the social hall.

Above: Sheep shearing at Port Howard
Opposite: Port Howard settlement

Snake plant – one of over 60 species here

PORT HOWARD: 51°37'S 59°31'W   Ownership: Port Howard Farming Ltd.   Size: 200,000 acres (80,940 ha)   Population: 30

SAUNDERS ISLAND

FEATURES

▸ Four species of breeding penguins: gentoo, king, Magellanic and rockhopper

▸ Black-browed albatross

▸ Dramatic scenery

▸ East of the north-facing beach, rockhoppers come ashore in incredible style. Claw markings can be seen in the rocks where these birds have been travelling to and from their colonies for thousands of years

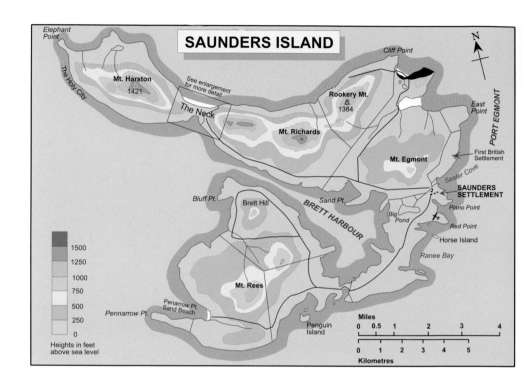

The rockhopper experience

INTRODUCTION

Saunders Island was named after the British Admiral Sir Charles Saunders who accompanied Lord Anson during his round the world voyage in the 1770's. In 1765 Port Egmont on Saunders Island was chosen as the site of the first British settlement on the Falkland Islands. Reasons included the presence of a safe natural harbour and nutritional plants that particularly benefited sailors travelling on long voyages.

SAUNDERS ISLAND: 51°22'S 60°05'W   **Ownership: Tony and David Pole-Evans**   **Size: 31,000 acres (12,545 ha)**   **Population: 7**

70

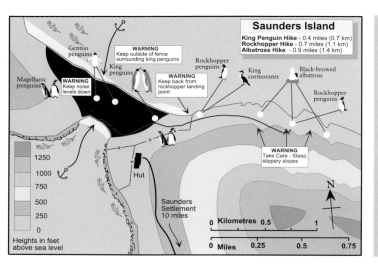

Saunders Island

King Penguin Hike - 0.4 miles (0.7 km)
Rockhopper Hike - 0.7 miles (1.1 km)
Albatross Hike - 0.9 miles (1.4 km)

Gentoo penguins

WARNING Keep outside of fence surrounding king penguins

King penguins

Rockhopper penguins

Magellanic penguins

WARNING Keep noise levels down

WARNING Keep back from rockhopper landing point

King cormorants

Black-browed albatross

Rockhopper penguins

1250
1000
750
500
250
0

Heights in feet above sea level

Hut

Saunders Settlement 10 miles

WARNING Take Care - Steep, slippery slopes

N

0 Kilometres 0.5 1

0 Miles 0.25 0.5 0.75

POINTERS

▸ During the hike towards Mount Richards care must be taken due to the steep slopes and the slippery grass.

▸ Be careful not to crowd the rockhoppers' landing spot.

▸ Take care not to disturb nesting Falkland skuas and oystercatchers; they nest in exposed scrapes of sand. The birds are particularly vulnerable between November and January.

▸ Do not walk through the gentoo colonies.

The Island was first leased for farming in the late 1800's and was bought by Tony and David Pole-Evans in 1987. Most of the seven people resident on Saunders Island have lived there all of their lives. Two of these are children and the travelling teacher visits every other month with the rest of the lessons being conducted by two-way radio and the telephone.

The clay airstrip is a short drive south from the settlement and it is visited, on average, once a day in the summer and once a week in winter. The plane brings mail, visitors and stores. The residents are almost self sufficient, growing all their own

Black-browed albatross clifftop colony (right) and weighing an albatross chick as part of the ongoing monitoring scheme by Falklands Conservation (top right)

vegetables and having a large herd of cattle for meat, milk and cream. The principal product is wool from a flock of 9,550 sheep on an island of 30,640 acres (12,400 ha). The island is still largely farmed in the traditional style although motorbikes and Land Rovers supplement the use of horses for stock work.

LANDINGS

Landings from the sea are generally made at The Neck, a narrow isthmus that links Elephant Point to the main part of the island. Depending on wind direction, landings are made on the north or south sandy beaches. The southerly beach is about 440 yds (400 m) long while the northerly beach is about 1 mile (1·6 km) long.

The Pole-Evans family greet visitors on landing. The Neck lies over 10 miles (16 km) from the Island's settlement, giving it an extra sense of isolation.

HIKE AND WILDLIFE

Saunders Island is the second largest offshore island within the Falkland Islands archipelago and is home to a rich diversity of wildlife, notably 11,000 breeding pairs of black-browed albatross and four different species of penguins.

To the west of The Neck lies Mount Harston which rises to 1421 ft (433 m), while the Island's highest point on Mount Richards 1500 ft (457 m), is located to the east. Zodiac journeys to The Neck attract groups of gentoo penguins that bob inquisitively in the water. Shorebirds seen on either side of The Neck include Magellanic and blackish oystercatchers, kelp geese and Falkland steamer ducks.

The hike from the southern beach circles the colonies of gentoo penguins nesting on the dark

Silvery grebe (below) and white-tufted grebe (below right) breed on Saunders Island

The view across The Neck, Saunders Island from Mount Harston

Example of a trypot

Rockhopper penguin claw marks

eroded area between the beaches, before heading for the northern shoreline. Always walk **around** the gentoo colonies and keep noise levels down. Please remember always to give these birds the right of way. If frightened on their way to the nest, they will return to the sea, possibly resulting in the loss of a vital meal for a hungry chick.

Hundreds of Magellanic penguins have their burrows in the soft soil on either side of The Neck. Care should be taken not to get too close, as the ground is fragile and liable to crumble. Don't forget, your floor may be a penguin's ceiling.

Penguin hunters frequented the Island, attracted by the abundance of breeding colonies. A trypot, once used for boiling down penguins for their oil, is still visible near the southern beach, providing a stark reminder of past persecution. Apparently, it took eight penguins to make 1 gallon (4·5 litres) of oil.

On the north-east side of The Neck there is a small but expanding colony of king penguins. These birds have been fenced off in order to reduce disturbance and to encourage breeding.

In 2000 The Neck supported 6,700 gentoos, and 20+ king penguins, while on the cliffs to the east 5,600 pairs of rockhopper penguins, 3,800 black-browed albatross and approximately 350 king cormorants were breeding.

The hike to the black-browed albatross, rockhopper and king cormorant colonies on the northern side of Mount Richards can be tough walking, with a climb of 300 ft (90 m) and a distance of about 1,100 yds (1 km), but it is well worth the effort. Please take your time, pause on the way, sit down and enjoy the magnificent view.

Despite the presence of rats on the Island there are some small birds to be seen, including dark-faced ground-tyrants and Falkland thrushes. These are mainly evident near the rockhopper colonies scavenging on flies or any titbits they can find. You may also be lucky enough to see striated caracaras preying on the upland geese. There are one or two pairs of crested caracara which are sometimes visible to the north-east around the albatross colonies or occasionally near the cabin.

VEGETATION

Most of Saunders Island is dry heath land with some notable flowering plants, including the striking silvery buttercup and the dainty hairy daisy which are both scarce endemics. All four of the native orchids are present, as is the attractive yellow pale maiden. Throughout the summer, from seashore to mountaintop, there are plenty of plants in flower to discover.

GEOLOGY

Possibly the most interesting geomorphology in this part of the island can be seen on the eroded peat slope near the gentoo penguin colonies. The drying and cracking of the peat, has produced interlocking polygons into which the wind has blown sand and small pebbles.

The high ground on this island is mostly underlain by hard, quartzite rock about 400 million years old. Slightly older, softer, yellowish-brown sandstone

underlies the lower parts of the Island. Some of these brown sandstones contain dark streaks, the remains of plants, and in a few places well-preserved fossil sea shells have been found. All the constituents were originally deposited at the margin of a shallow sea. The surrounding hills are made of quartz sandstones and their erosion over time has produced the white sand of the beaches. The sandstone also contains a scattering of pink garnet grains and whilst these are too sparsely distributed to be noticed in the rock, they also end up on the beach as sand grains. The garnet grains are denser, and so are heavier, than the vastly more abundant quartz grains which allows the action of wind and waves to winnow them out. Pink streaks and layers on the beach show where the garnet grains have been left behind when the lighter quartz grains were washed or blown away.

Some of the many plants to be discovered on Saunders Island. Clockwise from top left: Lady's slipper, the uncommon endemic silvery buttercup, pale maiden and the rare endemic hairy daisy

75

SEA LION ISLAND

FEATURES
- Three breeding species of penguins (rockhopper, gentoo and Magellanic)
- Very large breeding site of southern elephant seals
- Killer whale pods regularly observed close to the eastern landing beaches
- Extensive tussac grass stands and ungrazed heathland
- Ponds with numerous waterfowl and waders
- At least 40 species of birds with good possibilities of spotting vagrants
- Breeding colony of southern sea lions
- Easy walking terrain

Peale's dolphin

INTRODUCTION
Sea Lion Island lies 10 miles (16 km) south of mainland East Falkland. The Island is a relatively flat plateau with perpendicular cliffs of 80 ft (24 m) towards the south-western point, lower cliffs on the northern coast and a sandy isthmus linking a rocky bluff to the east with the main island. It has a total area of 2,236 acres (905 ha) and is owned by the Falkland Islands Development Corporation. The Island has the most southerly British hotel in the world, which is privately owned.

Sea Lion Island was originally a sheep farm and the farmhouse was built from an old sailing shipwreck, the British vessel *Viscount*, which was wrecked here in 1892. Due to the wool market decline and a wish to protect the ecology of the Island, most sheep have been removed and subsequently the grasses have thrived. This has provided better cover for small birds such as the Magellanic snipe, rufous-chested dotterel, the endemic Cobb's wren and the Falkland grass wren. Fortunately Sea Lion Island is free of cats, rats and mice introduced unwittingly to many other parts of the Falkland Islands. It has been selected for designation as a National Nature Reserve and as a Ramsar Site (see Glossary).

LANDINGS
Zodiac landings on Sea Lion Island are very dependent on weather and sea conditions. Landings take place towards the eastern point on the north or south side of the isthmus on to sandy beaches, also on the northern side to the west of the settlement. These wet landings are extremely exposed due to the prevailing westerly winds in the islands.

HIKE – WILDLIFE – VEGETATION
The most commonly seen dolphins are Peale's, which are often attracted to the sound of the Zodiac engine. If you are lucky, pods of killer whales can be observed circling close to shore, attracted by the prospect of penguins and seals. In February 2001 a juvenile killer whale became stranded on one of the landing beaches. A small team of people worked for two hours eventually

Rufous-chested dotterel

SEA LION ISLAND: 52°26'S 59°05'W   Ownership: Falkland Islands Development Corporation   Size: 2,236 acres (905 ha)   Population: 5

76

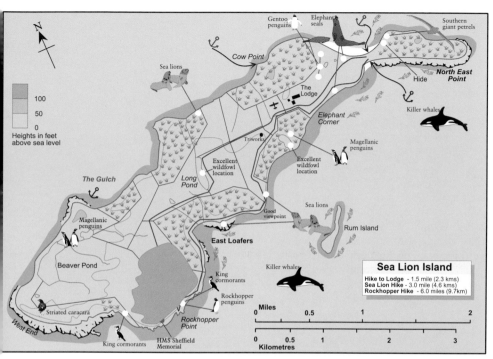

Sea Lion Island

Hike to Lodge - 1.5 mile (2.3 kms)
Sea Lion Hike - 3.0 mile (4.6 kms)
Rockhopper Hike - 6.0 miles (9.7km)

Heights in feet above sea level

100
50
0

Gentoo penguins
Elephant seals
Cow Point
Sea lions
The Lodge
Hide
North East Point
Killer whales
Southern giant petrels
Elephant Corner
Triworks
Magellanic penguins
Excellent wildfowl location
Excellent wildfowl location
The Gulch
Long Pond
Magellanic penguins
Good viewpoint
Sea lions
Rum Island
East Loafers
Beaver Pond
Killer whales
King cormorants
Rockhopper penguins
Striated caracara
West End
King cormorants
HMS Sheffield Memorial
Rockhopper Point

Miles
0   0.5   1   2

0   0.5   1   2   3
Kilometres

Male elephant seal (above)
A group of elephant seals bask on a beach (below)

POINTERS

▸ Use the wooden hide provided when observing the southern giant petrels.

▸ Be vigilant when walking through tussac grass areas, wary of the sea lions and elephant seals lurking within. Try to walk on the landward side.

▸ Be aware of nesting birds in the long grasses such as snipe, short-eared owls and Falkland skuas.

▸ There are extensive kelp beds on approach to all landings. All landings are subject to swell and surf.

▸ Cruise ship staff must check with the Lodge Manager, before using the facilities. There is a small shop at which USD and some credit cards are accepted. All visitors are welcome. Contact can be made on VHF channel 16.

freeing the youngster. The story goes that the mother swam by and flicked her tail, in thanks for the team's efforts.

Elephant Corner to the south-east has large stands of tussac grass. A leisurely stroll to Elephant Corner along the sandy beaches takes in the black-throated finches and the ever-present tussacbirds. Elephant seals on both the northern and southern beaches form the largest population in the archipelago, approximately 2,000 individuals at the height of the breeding season (560 breeding females). The main pupping period is in October/November. Pups put on 9 lb (5 kg) in body weight per day on their mother's rich milk. It is important to remain at least two or three animal lengths away, but remember not to get between them and the sea. Adult male elephant seals are also ashore from mid December to April when they moult. Their agility often surprises (as does their foul breath) even though they can grow up to 15 ft (4·5 m) long and weigh up to 3·5 tonnes. Approximately 70 southern sea lions use this beach under the southern cliffs to the west of Elephant Corner and have about 60 pups a year.

There is a small number of breeding southern giant petrels on Sea Lion Island. The colony is situated at the northern landing site on the beach to the east of the Island. Giant petrels are habitual ship followers and have a wingspan of two metres so keep an eye out when approaching the Island. They are locally named 'stinkers' due to their habit of vomiting and spitting when disturbed at the

Male southern sea lion

Tussacbird

nest, so you have been warned. Petrels are extremely sensitive to interference and will abandon eggs or young if they are disturbed, so please use the hide provided.

Situated on the peaty mounds between the two eastern landing beaches are 2,800 breeding pairs of gentoo penguins. Watching their behaviour is entertaining and these birds in particular are extremely curious and will probably approach you, especially if you sit down and remain quiet.

The hike to Rockhopper Point to the west is about 3 miles (4·8 km). There are approximately 480 pairs of rockhoppers and a large king cormorant nesting site along the cliffs in this area, which stretches 750 yds (0·7 km) up the coastline. Nesting rock cormorants are visible on an impressive arch, where the sea has pounded the cliffs over the centuries.

At Bull Hill, which is approximately 150 ft (46 m) high, a memorial has been erected to the

Tussac grass on Sea Lion Island

crew of HMS *Sheffield*, the British warship sunk by Argentine Forces in 1982. The terrain provides generally easy walking on heath land with extensive areas of cinnamon grass, the scent of which can fill the air on a calm day. An estimated 70 species of flowering plants have been recorded on the Island, including the endemics vanilla daisy and coastal nassauvia, and the Fuegian yellow violet. The areas of tussac grassland have been protected from overgrazing and cover large parts of the southern coastline. They are alive with thrushes, finches, tussacbirds and Magellanic penguins. You should see the endemic Cobb's wren. The southern tussac paddock also provides a good viewpoint for the southern sea lion breeding area.

There are abundant breeding pairs of Magellanic penguins on the Island, mainly situated on the greens and in tussac areas. Watch out for their burrows and for resting southern sea lions lying low within the tussac. Sea Lion Island has at least six breeding pairs of striated caracaras which represent about one percent of the Falklands' total population. Crested caracaras may also be seen on this hike, though there is probably only one resident pair.

Summer months provide a challenge to the water level of the Island, with the various centrally located winter ponds virtually disappearing between November and early March. Waterfowl can be seen on the two ponds heading west towards Rockhopper Point including Chiloë wigeon, speckled and silver teal and Patagonian crested duck. On Long Pond there is a notable stand of the tall California club-rush, which is frequented by a small colony of silvery grebes. Wading birds to be seen while crossing the open heathland include rufous-chested dotterel, two-banded plover and the white-rumped sandpiper, a non-breeding visitor in September to mid April from Arctic Canada.

GEOLOGY

Gently inclined beds of sandstone and mudstone make up this Island. The rocks were originally deposited as layers of sand and mud in a very large, deep lake about 250 million years ago. On some of the mudstone beds thin, meandering lines can be seen. These are the traces made by soft-bodied animals and possibly fish, as they grazed across the muddy lakebed.

*Pods of killer whale or orc
are seen regularly clos
offshor*

The diversity of Sea Lion Island: King cormorants at rock platform resting place (above), Magellanic penguins gathered by a pond (below) and a close up of kelp (right)

STEEPLE JASON

Tony Chater

FEATURES

▸ The largest black-browed albatross colony in the world (157,000)

▸ Large numbers of striated caracaras and Falkland skuas

▸ Large numbers of nesting southern giant petrels

▸ Be sure to bring enough camera film: the scenery is breathtaking

Vanilla daisy

INTRODUCTION

The Jasons are a knobbly chain of reef-strewn, tide-ripped islands which stretch 40 miles (64 km) north and west off West Falkland towards Patagonia. Grand and Steeple Jason rise dramatically to around 1,000 ft (305 m) and may well have been the first of the islands in the Falklands sighted by Europeans during their pioneering voyages to the southern oceans in the 16th century.

The Jason Islands were originally known as the Sebaldines, after the Dutch navigator Sebald de Weert, who recorded sighting them in 1600. They were re-named the Jason Islands in 1766 by Captain John Macbride who had been sent by the British Admiralty to survey the Falklands in the frigate HMS *Jason*. Steeple Jason belongs to the Wildlife Conservation Society, New York. They help to preserve outstanding wildlife habitats in 52 countries.

Steeple Jason itself is, arguably, the most dramatic of all the islands in the archipelago. With the exception of two low-lying outliers, Jason East Cay and Jason West Cay, it is also the most westerly. Steeple Jason is 6 miles (10 km) long and 1 mile (1·6 km) across and lies northwest to southeast. It has a total land area of 1,952 acres (790 ha). From the coasts the land rises steeply to a rocky ridge which runs along its length except where the

island is divided almost in half by a low-lying and very narrow neck.

The vast number of birds on this island were quickly noticed by early human visitors and during the 18th and 19th centuries, many thousands of penguins were rounded up, clubbed and rendered down for their oil. Remnants of this not so long extinct industry, such as large rusting trypots, can still be found in sheltered bays where it would have been easier to land a boat. Further evidence lies on the southern part of the neck where countless penguin

STEEPLE JASON: 51°02'S 61°12'W at the central neck   Ownership: Wildlife Conservation Society   Size: 1,952 acres (790 ha)   Population: 0

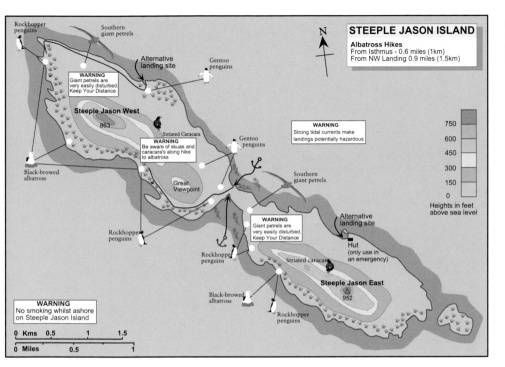

STEEPLE JASON ISLAND

Albatross Hikes
From Isthmus - 0.6 miles (1km)
From NW Landing 0.9 miles (1.5km)

Rockhopper penguins

Southern giant petrels

Alternative landing site

Gentoo penguins

WARNING
Giant petrels are very easily disturbed. Keep Your Distance

Steeple Jason West

863

Striated Caracara

WARNING
Be aware of skuas and caracara's along hike to albatross

Gentoo penguins

WARNING
Strong tidal currents make landings potentially hazardous

Black-browed albatross

Great Viewpoint

Southern giant petrels

Rockhopper penguins

WARNING
Giant petrels are very easily disturbed. Keep Your Distance

Alternative landing site

Hut
(only use in an emergency)

Rockhopper penguins

Striated caracara

Steeple Jason East
952

Black-browed albatross

Rockhopper penguins

WARNING
No smoking whilst ashore on Steeple Jason Island

0 Kms 0.5 1 1.5
0 Miles 0.5 1

750
600
450
300
150
0
Heights in feet above sea level

Dolphin gull

bones and skulls can be found scattered on the bare ground. For a century, from 1872 onwards, around 800 sheep were grazed on the Steeple. The declining wool markets brought an end to this operation and the remaining livestock were slaughtered in 1968. Some of the fencing and the old shearing shed are still standing. Today both Steeple and neighbouring Grand Jason are uninhabited nature reserves.

A word of warning: Falklands weather is notoriously changeable and this island in particular is girdled by exceptionally strong tidal currents. There are no recognised harbours. If the wind should change or increase dramatically it may be necessary to abort the landing at short notice due to sea conditions so please

POINTERS
‣ The landings can be difficult due to the exposed coastline. Zodiac drivers must beware of submerged rocks and swell.
‣ Staff need to be carefully posted to assist visitors in rocky areas, especially along the north western shoreline.
‣ Do not smoke on this island; there is an extremely high fire risk.

Coastal nassauvia – a widespread endemic cushion-forming plant

Grass wren

pay particular attention to the advice of your guides.

LANDINGS – WILDLIFE – VEGETATION

Cruise ship visitors generally land on either the north or south side of the neck depending on weather and wind conditions in particular. Once ashore it is a fairly short walk to the world's largest black-browed albatross colony, containing approximately 157,000 breeding pairs. The main part of the colony is 218 yds (200 m) wide and stretches for a staggering 3 miles (5 km) along the south-western seaboard of Steeple Jason West. It is flanked on the landward side by a border of dense and largely impenetrable tussac grass. Amongst the albatross are nesting rockhopper penguins (about 89,760 pairs) and king cormorants. Pairs of striated caracaras nest in remarkable proximity to each other along the tussac verges and many of the smaller passerine species can also be seen. Falkland skuas also breed here in large numbers and both they and the caracaras can be very aggressive and may attack you in defence of their territories. Beware and avoid invading their space. Also, quite a substantial gentoo penguin colony is located near to the landing area.

An alternative landing area is in a gully half way along the north facing shore of Steeple Jason West. This landing may be more awkward for elderly visitors but provides closer access to the main albatross colony at the north-west end. The tussac is virtually impenetrable around the colony so the route goes along the boulder beach on the northern shore. It is a fair distance along this beach and care should be taken not to turn an ankle on the loose rocks. The reward is a quite awesome view of part of the world's greatest albatross colony. You may also come across some massive and partially overgrown ship's timbers. These are from an unknown vessel which was wrecked here, probably in the 19th century. There are a small number of South American fur seals on the north-western tip of the Island. They are rather shy so approach them with due care.

Since the Island became a sanctuary in 1970, Steeple Jason is gradually recovering from overgrazing by sheep, although there are extensive areas of erosion on the steeper slopes, with little growing apart from sheep's sorrel and some cushion plants. Tussac grass is again thriving inshore of the albatross colonies and in places reaches at least 500 ft (150 m) on the southwestern slopes of the crags. Cushions of emerald-bog and coastal nassauvia are common and the two Falkland ragworts also occur. Vanilla daisy, lady's slipper and a total of about 40 species of flowering plants have been found, including four endemics.

There are a number of breeding groups of southern giant petrels or stinkers, the largest of all the petrels. If you come across a colony please keep well away because they are easily disturbed and will often leave their nests and fly upon sighting a human being. They take quite a long time before returning. This leaves the chicks or eggs vulnerable to opportunistic attack by the caracaras or skuas. If you approach a giant petrel colony too closely you will almost certainly cause major disruption and loss of bird life.

GEOLOGY

The Jasons poke out of the ocean like the giant vertebrae of a drowned sea monster and are formed geologically by a large pair of folds, now mostly submerged under the ocean. Steeple Jason, in common with most of the Jason Islands group, is made up of hard quartz sandstone more than 400 million years old. The beds of rock were originally laid down as horizontal layers of sand under the shallow water at the margin of a large sea. Since then the rock beds have been tilted and are now steeply inclined towards the south-west. In a few places the traces of thin, pipe-like structures can be seen in the rock perpendicular to the bed layers. These are the remains of tube-worm burrows, the final vestige of the original inhabitants of the ancient sea floor.

Part of the largest black-browed albatross colony in the world

VOLUNTEER POINT

FEATURES
▸ King penguin colony (1000+ birds)
▸ Beautiful sand beach
▸ Plentiful bird life
▸ Southern sea lions are often to be seen feeding on penguins near the shore

Falkland thrush

INTRODUCTION
Volunteer Point, an impressive peninsula to the north-east of Berkeley Sound, is named after the ship *Volunteer* in which Captain Edmund Fanning called at Port Louis in 1815. It is part of Johnsons Harbour Farm, which runs 15,000 sheep and was established in 1870 by George Patterson Smith. The farm has remained in the same family and it is one of the few surviving large farms in the Falkland Islands. Volunteer Point is 10 miles (16 km) from the farm settlement and a four hour overland drive from Stanley. This tests the skill of most drivers due to the softness of the wet peat over which the track runs.

LANDING AND WILDLIFE
When ocean swells permit, the most popular landing site on the peninsula is the 2 miles (3·2 km) long Volunteer Beach. This impressive strip of white sand is bordered by a high grass bank, leading down to rolling greens, which provide the ideal habitat for three species of penguin: gentoo, Magellanic and king.

Volunteer Point has 770 breeding pairs of gentoo penguin and many hundreds of pairs of Magellanic penguins. It is also the Falklands' most successful breeding ground for king penguins. At the last count in 2000/2001, there were at least 500 breeding pairs and 260 chicks. Due to their breeding cycle there are chicks all year round, so caution is needed. These colonies are situated on the greens to the south, approximately 300 yds (275 m) from the landing beach. This hike involves a gentle climb of less than 75 ft (23 m).

To the south, a number of gentoo colonies can be seen on a slight ridge. The acidity of the guano produced by these colonies has resulted in large circular patches of dead turf, evident because the colonies tend to move their sites slightly each year. The greens of Volunteer Point are dotted with Magellanic penguin burrows in both directions along the coastline.

Set back from Volunteer Beach, to the north of Volunteer Lagoon, is Volunteer Shanty, a small traditional shepherd's house dating from the 1960's. The house paddock contains the foundations of an older shanty built in 1877, and a small stand of

Flowers of the edible teaberry

VOLUNTEER POINT: 51°28'S 57°50'W at the shanty   **Ownership: Smith brothers**   **Size: 36,000 acres (14,570 ha)**   **Population: 7**

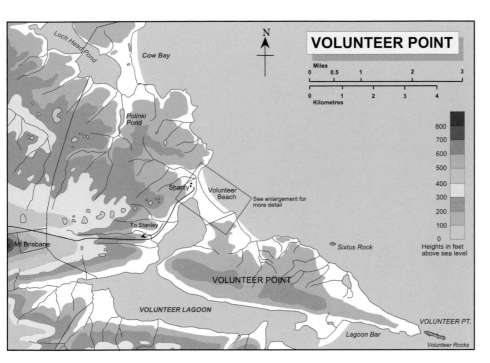

VOLUNTEER POINT

Heights in feet above sea level

See enlargement for more detail

Fachine

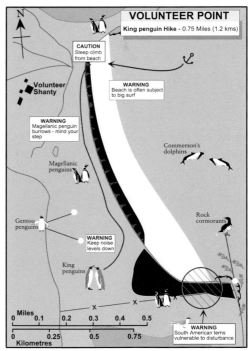

VOLUNTEER POINT

King penguin Hike - 0.75 Miles (1.2 kms)

CAUTION
Steep climb from beach

WARNING
Beach is often subject to big surf

Volunteer Shanty

WARNING
Magellanic penguin burrows - mind your step

Commerson's dolphins

Magellanic penguins

Gentoo penguins

WARNING
Keep noise levels down

King penguins

Rock cormorants

WARNING
South American terns vulnerable to disturbance

POINTERS

▸ The climb from the landing beach to the greens and the penguins can be tricky due to very soft sand.

▸ Do not get between penguins returning from the sea to their colony. This can create panic and cause birds to regurgitate food collected for their chicks.

▸ Do not approach kings whilst incubating an egg on their feet. They can be easily disturbed and the egg lost.

conifers that provide shelter to a number of introduced European rabbits. Interestingly, the sheep pens built in this area are made from driftwood from the wreck of the *Sixtus,* which hit a large rock just off the mainland in 1905.

Small birds seen in this area include long-tailed meadowlarks, Falkland thrushes, Magellanic snipe, Falkland pipits, and dark-faced ground-tyrants. Over 40 bird species have been recorded, including rock cormorant, South American tern, blackish and Magellanic oystercatchers, dolphin and kelp gulls, upland, kelp and ruddy-headed geese .

VEGETATION
Despite the continual trampling of hundreds of penguin feet, there are interesting plants to discover at Volunteer Point, especially as you move away from the main penguin colonies. During the summer a feature of the beaches is the sea cabbage, with silvery grey leaves crowned by distinctive yellow flowers. In grassy places near the sea look for the little delicate pink flowers of pimpernel.

Near the shanty there are patches of fachine and during January these bushes are covered in hundreds of white daisy-like flower heads. These were used by South American Indians to restore eyesight and as an eyewash. Elsewhere, dwarf shrub heath and whitegrass plains can be seen. There are also carpets of what is locally termed cushion-bog, among which the red, sticky, leaves of the carnivorous sundew can be found. In February, teaberries are ripe. This pale-pink, aromatic-tasting fruit is locally collected for eating fresh or baking in cakes and buns, which are delicious.

Flying steamer duck; female with duckling (below left) and Falkland flightless steamer duck; adult male (below right). Both species have been seen in the Volunteer Point area.

GEOLOGY

The rocks forming this headland are hard quartz-sandstones. They are among the oldest of the Falklands' sedimentary rock units and started their existence as sand beds deposited in shallower water at the margin of a large sea.

The beaches in this part of the Islands contain unusual pebbles; rounded fragments of agate known as "Falkland Pebbles" and ranging in colour from translucent white to deep red. Their origin is mysterious since no rock of that type occurs within the *in situ* geological sequence. The pebbles are collected and polished to produce local jewellery.

The striking long-tailed meadowlark

Three of the king penguins that frequent the Volunteer Point area

King cormorants

Rock cormorant

WEDDELL ISLAND

FEATURES
▸ Stroll to gentoo and Magellanic penguins colonies
▸ Weddell Inn
▸ Hike up Mt Weddell provides superb views
▸ Landings may be achieved at Loop Head or any of the beautiful beaches.

Weddell Island, which used to be called Swan Island, is the third largest island within the Falklands and is named after Captain James Weddell, the Antarctic explorer. It was first leased in 1871 and in the early days was overstocked and overgrazed, once having 23,500 sheep. The numbers of sheep have declined over the years and the vegetation is beginning to recover. There are now only 400 sheep, a small herd of cattle and some wild horses.

The Patagonian fox was introduced in 1926 both for its fur and in an attempt to keep the upland goose population down. At the time it was believed that geese ruined the grazing ground for sheep by competing for the rich green grass. For many years Government paid a bounty on these birds through an official known as the Collector of Goose Beaks. However the introduction of the foxes proved to be disastrous as they supplemented their diet with lambs.

John Hamilton, one time owner of the Island, also experimented in processing seals for their oil in 1923. Samples of oil sent to Britain proved to be suitable as a base for paint. However, a trial in which 384 sea lions were boiled down produced only 11 barrels of oil and the venture was deemed a failure in 1925/6. Some small stone-walled pens that were used for holding seals can still be seen on the Island.

The Weddell Inn

Patagonian crested duck

Landings at the settlement are made either by using the wooden jetty or the rocky shoreline in the sheltered Gull Harbour. Directly in front of the landing area is Weddell Inn, where everyone is welcome.

The hike to the gentoo penguins on Mark Point is 1 mile (1·6 km), and the fairly level terrain makes for easy walking. Magellanic penguin burrows are prolific along the coastline of this point.

Chiloë wigeon and Patagonian crested duck can be seen on a small pond close to the gentoo colonies. Falkland pipits can be seen in the long grass. Turkey vultures, striated caracaras and Falkland skuas can be observed circling above these penguin colonies. A total of 33 bird species has recently been recorded within $2\frac{1}{2}$ miles (4 km) of the settlement. More than 100 plant species were recorded in October 2000, including whitlowgrass at Loop Head and the largest concentration known of endemic silvery buttercup near Kelp Creek. Both of these

WEDDELL ISLAND: 51°54'S 60°54'W at Inn   Ownership: Strachan Visick Ltd.   Size: 54,000 acres (21,850 ha)   Population: 3

populations are likely to be of national importance due to their size and extent.

For the more adventurous and fitter, Mount Weddell 1,256 ft (383 m) can be climbed, providing absolutely stunning views. There is a visitors book to be signed at the summit.

Weddell Island scenery, fauna and flora:
Tidal creek and gorse at the settlement (above); Dark-faced ground-tyrant
(top right); whitlowgrass (far right) and Falkland pipit (right)

WEST POINT ISLAND

FEATURES
▶ Tea with Roddy and Lily Napier
▶ Black-browed albatross
▶ Rockhopper and Magellanic penguins
▶ The Devil's Nose and surrounding cliffs
▶ Beautiful scenery
▶ Settlement and gardens circled by striated caracara and turkey vultures

The inquisitive johnny rook

INTRODUCTION

West Point Island lies off the most north-westerly point of mainland West Falkland and is 3,100 acres (1,255 ha). The attractive settlement sits on the edge of a small harbour on the eastern side of the Island, in the lee of Black Bog Hill and Michael's Mount. The valley between these two peaks rolls over the centre of the Island to the dramatic Devil's Nose, one of the Island's main attractions. From here visitors are treated to splendid views of Cliff Mountain, the Island's highest point at 1,250 ft (381m), and the highest cliffs in the Falklands.

The Island was formerly known as Albatross Island. Eighteenth century sealers, who are thought to be the first visitors, probably applied this name. It quickly became a principal base for sealing operations. In 1820-21 the sailing ship *General Knox* from Salem, Massachusetts, spent almost two years moored in West Point harbour, receiving seal skins from the sloop *Penguin* which hunted around West Falkland. Sealers and wild cattle largely destroyed the Island's healthy tussac, which had grown along the northern coastline. The sealers planted gardens reporting that potatoes grew well, thus providing fresh supplies of vegetables for themselves. In his diary of the Voyage of HMS *Lady Nelson*, Lt. James Grant wrote of West Point Island in January 1802:

The new landing ramp

"Celery I found plentiful growing here, and for scurvy, common dock with boiled cabbage. Potatoes were taken to sea and eaten raw."

West Point Island was first leased to Arthur Felton to farm sheep in 1879. He found the remains of a small stone hut, which still stands in the settlement today, and is thought to be the only remnant of the sealing era. This was Arthur's home. He had only enough money for one building project and he decided that the shearing shed took priority over a house. He began an extensive tussac-replanting programme and by 1910 had replanted almost the whole northern coastline. In fact Arthur was so ahead of his time with the notion of tussac replanting, he was thought locally to be quite mad. Tussac planting has continued for many years with the island now having several healthy plantations. The present owners are also enthusiastic tree planters, as can be seen in the settlement and to the west of the harbour.

The lease and ownership of West Point Island has always been in the possession of Arthur Felton and

WEST POINT ISLAND: 51°21'S 60°41'W   **Ownership: Roddy and Lily Napier**   **Size: 2,700 acres (1,255 ha)**   **Population: 2**

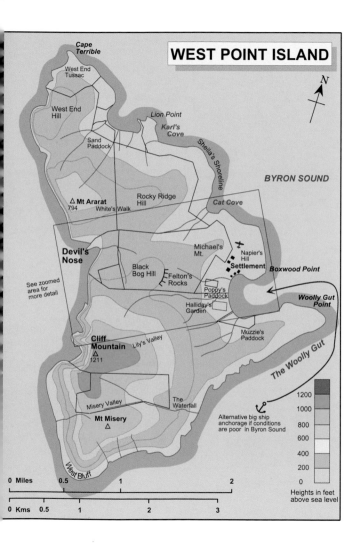

WEST POINT ISLAND

Cape Terrible
West End Tussac
West End Hill
Lion Point
Karl's Cove
Sand Paddock
Sheila's Shoreline
BYRON SOUND
Rocky Ridge Hill
△ Mt Ararat 794
White's Walk
Cat Cove
Devil's Nose
Michael's Mt.
Napier's Hill
Settlement
Boxwood Point
See zoomed area for more detail
Black Bog Hill
Felton's Rocks
Poppy's Paddock
Woolly Gut Point
Halliday's Garden
Muzzie's Paddock
Cliff Mountain △ 1211
Lily's Valley
The Woolly Gut
Misery Valley
The Waterfall
Mt Misery △
Alternative big ship anchorage if conditions are poor in Byron Sound
West Bluff

1200
1000
800
600
400
200
0
Heights in feet above sea level

0 Miles 0.5 1 2
0 Kms 0.5 1 2 3

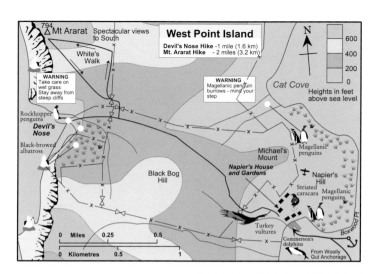

West Point Island
Devil's Nose Hike -1 mile (1.6 km)
Mt. Ararat Hike - 2 miles (3.2 km)

794 △ Mt Ararat Spectacular views to South
White's Walk
WARNING Take care on wet grass Stay away from steep cliffs
WARNING Magellanic penguin burrows - mind your step
Cat Cove
Heights in feet above sea level
Rockhopper penguins
Devil's Nose
Black-browed albatross
Michael's Mount
Magellanic penguins
Black Bog Hill
Napier's House and Gardens
Napier's Hill
Striated caracara
Magellanic penguins
Turkey vultures
Commerson's dolphins
From Woolly Gut Anchorage
Boxwood Pt

600
400
200
0

0 Miles 0.25 0.5
0 Kilometres 0.5 1

Lily and Roddy Napier

POINTERS

▸ The hike is moderately strenuous. Please accept the offer of transport if needed. The return hike is much easier than the outward leg.

▸ Be careful when making your descent to the Devil's Nose. The short spiky grass can be wet and slippery.

▸ Absolutely no smoking ashore please. The land and vegetation is very dry in the summer and fire is a serious hazard.

Arthur Felton

his descendants. His niece, Gladys 'Muzzie' Napier, bought the island in 1959 and subsequently passed ownership on to her son Roddy. He and his wife, Lily, still run West Point Island as a traditional sheep farm, milking cows and growing their own vegetables. They are representatives of a rugged and independent way of island life, which is sadly disappearing in the Falkland Islands.

Islander aircraft of the Falkland Islands Government Air Service bring stores and mail periodically, landing on a grass airstrip near the settlement. This is one of the most weather-dependent airstrips in the Falklands, and during bad weather the service quite often has to be cancelled, especially in the winter. This does not particularly bother the Napiers, who leave the island, "as little as possible". Medical help comes in the form of a flying doctor. Roddy claims it was once seven years before they needed to see one.

It is a tribute to the Napiers and their enduring hospitality that the ashes of Lars-Eric Lindblad lie under a mass of the endemic Felton's flower in their garden. Lars-Eric, who can truly be regarded as the father of Falkland Islands tourism, brought the *Navarino* to West Point in 1968, the first cruise vessel to visit the Islands. This visit led to many others and the development of firm and lasting friendships.

LANDING

The landing site is in the sheltered harbour just below the settlement. There are some small kelp beds in the bay, but these provide little or no obstacle for Zodiacs and tenders. The landing is either 'dry' using one of

The endemic Felton's flower

the two jetties, or 'wet' if opting for the sand and pebble beach. However, the recently built wooden landing ramp will provide a dry landing at all states of the tide. A variety of buildings exist in this immediate area, some of which are over 125 years old. The remains of a vessel called the *Redwing*, beached in 1993 during a terrific easterly gale, can be seen to the north of the landing site, below the shearing shed.

The bay is quite often literally teeming with Peale's dolphins wanting to play with the Zodiacs. Magellanic penguins nest in underground homes all around the harbour. Your landing on West Point may well be observed by a very rare and remarkably curious raptor, which can often be seen perched on buildings around the landing site. These are striated caracaras, one of the rarest birds of prey in the world. Several pairs breed at West Point and the island is a favourite haunt for many non-breeders. These fascinating birds often follow and observe walkers as they make their way across the island.

HIKE AND WILDLIFE

The main destination for most visitors is the Devil's Nose. This rocky promontory, which juts out into the sea in dramatic fashion from a spectacular coastline of steep cliffs, is an exhilarating habitat for some 2,100 breeding pairs of black-browed albatross, (the island has a total albatross population of 14,500 pairs). There are about 500 pairs of rockhopper penguins at the Devil's Nose. Combined with the surrounding precipices and abundant wildlife, it makes for one of the most breathtaking sites in the Falkland Islands. Visitors should look out for vagrants such as the grey-headed albatross, recorded on several occasions. The hike over to the Devil's Nose is $1\frac{1}{4}$ miles (2·2 km) long. The highest altitude of about 350 ft (107 m) is reached north of Black Bog Hill about half a mile (800 m) west of the jetty. This rounded hill overlooks the large peat bog to the north.

Hiking shoes/boots are fine for the walk, but rubber boots are more suitable when negotiating the tall tussac grass around the bird colonies at the Devil's Nose. For those not wishing to walk, Roddy and Lily will happily provide a cross-country ride in one of their eight-seater Land Rovers. The drive takes about ten minutes. They normally operate a continuous shuttle service for non-walkers. Following a visit to the Devil's Nose, visitors are offered a traditional Falkland Islands tea in the farmhouse. Don't miss this chance to sample the fine home-baked cakes in Lily's kitchen. This delightfully rambling building, the oldest part of which was built in 1880, is set in sheltered, long established gardens, which simply beg to be explored. The macrocarpa trees around the house are a favourite roost for turkey vultures. Typically a very timid bird, they display remarkable tameness in this particular environment.

VEGETATION

The walking is easy on short, grazed turf in which several attractive carpet-forming plants can be found. These include two endemics: the grey and green clubmoss cudweed and the dark green, prickly coastal nassauvia with scented creamy flowers in summer. Flat, fernlike leaf rosettes of Hooker's sweet

The settlement, West Point Island

cicely and the blue-white lopsided flowers of creeping berry-lobelia may also be found on the slopes. Excellent views and photo opportunities are possible, particularly looking southwards along the magnificent western cliffs and eastwards towards the West Falkland mainland.

GEOLOGY

The rocks of this island are mostly hard, white quartzite, about 400 million years old. They originated as layers of sand beneath the shallow water at the margins of a large sea. Two unusual occurrences here tell us something about the more recent history of the Falklands.

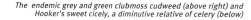
The endemic grey and green clubmoss cudweed (above right) and Hooker's sweet cicely, a diminutive relative of celery (below)

97

Left to right; two-banded plover (adult), a large nestling black-browed albatross; rockhopper penguins

Firstly, many sub-fossil bird bones have been found within a peat bog on the way to Devil's Nose. Since 1996, systematic collection has yielded about 500 specimens and close examination of bones after preservation has shown about two-thirds of them are bones of the striated caracara. Others originated from about 20 species of seabirds and landbirds, most still occurring in the Falklands. Samples of these bones have been radio-carbon dated at least 5,300 years old, by far the oldest evidence of birds yet found in the archipelago.

Secondly, hidden beneath the landing beach, directly in front of the settlement, is an accumulation of fossil trees. Bark and delicate twigs are still preserved so the possibility of a driftwood accumulation is unlikely. The material is probably several million years old and shows that at that time the Falkland Islands flora included trees.

GLOSSARY OF TERMS

Although not all mentioned in the Guide these are some slightly unusual terms quite regularly used by people living in the Falklands Islands.

Bogged	A vehicle stuck in the soft ground
Camp	Anywhere outside of Stanley
Chay	Friend or mate (derived from the Spanish term, Ché)
Corral	An enclosure for confining horses or cattle
Goose wing	The wing of an Upland Goose was often used as a brush for the ash around a peat fire/stove
Lafonia	The area of East Falkland south of the isthmus of Choiseul Sound
Ramsar	The International Convention for the Protection of Wetlands, particularly as habitat for waterfowl. So-called after the town in Iran where the first meeting of parties was held. A Ramsar site is internationally recognised as important for wetland birds and waterfowl. It must hold either 1% of the population, or be distinct in terms of its biodiversity, or be representative of a biogeographical area to qualify as such a site. **(There are 4 sites pending designation in the Falklands)**
Settlement	Collection of houses and buildings on a farm within the Falklands
Shanty	A shepherd's house away from the settlement
Smoko	Tea time, usually in the morning
Stone run	A mass of loose angular rock debris, formed by a number of different periglacial processes
Trypot	Structure, used a long time ago, for boiling penguins for their oil

ACRONYMS

The Falkland Islands seem to be ruled by long terms of initials. Below are some of the most commonly used to save some confusion for those of you arriving in the Islands.

FC	Falklands Conservation
FIC	Falkland Islands Company
FIGAS	Falkland Islands Government Air Service
MPA	Mount Pleasant Airfield
FIPASS	Falkland Islands Interim Port and Storage System
FIG	Falkland Islands Government
FITB	Falkland Islands Tourist Board
FIDC	Falkland Islands Development Corporation
FIBS	Falkland Islands Broadcasting Station
BFBS	British Forces Broadcasting Service
FICZ	Falkland Islands Interim Conservation and Management Zone
FOCZ	Falkland Islands Outer Fishery Conservation Zone

FURTHER READING

GENERAL READING

Corrals and Gauchos. Joan Spruce. Peregrine Publishing, Bangor. 1992. ISBN 1-873406-01-0.

Darwin's Desolate Islands. Patrick Armstrong. Picton Publishing, Chippenham. 1992. ISBN 0-948251-55-7.

Place Names of the Falkland Islands. Richard Munro. Bluntisham Books, Huntingdon. 1998. ISBN 1-871999-09-X.

The Falkland Islands. Ian J. Strange. David & Charles, Newton Abbot. 1985. ISBN 0-715385-31-3.

The Falkland Islands. Reading the Rocks – a geological travelogue. Phil Stone and Don Aldiss. British Geological Survey for Department of Mineral Resources, Falkland Islands Government. NERC and FIG. 2000. ISBN 0-852723-71-7.

The Falklands. Tony Chater. Penna Press, St Albans. 1993. ISBN 0-9504113-1-0.

Those Were The Days. John Smith. Bluntisham Books, Huntingdon. 1989. ISBN 1-871999-01-4.

MARITIME

Condemned at Stanley. John Smith. Picton Publishing, Chippenham. 1985. ISBN 0-948251-11-5.

Falkland Islands Shores. Ewen Southby-Tailyour. Conway Maritime, London. 1985. ISBN 0-85177-341-9.

NATURAL HISTORY

Albatrosses. W. L. N. Tickell. Pica Press, Sussex. 2000. ISBN 1-873403-94-1.

Atlas of Breeding Birds of the Falkland Islands. Robin W. & Anne Woods. Anthony Nelson, Oswestry. 1997. ISBN 0-904614-60-3.

Field Guide to the Wildlife of the Falkland Islands and South Georgia. Ian J. Strange. HarperCollins, London. 1992. ISBN 0-00-219839-8.

Flowering Plants of the Falkland Islands. Robin W. Woods. Falklands Conservation, London. 2000. ISBN 0-9538371-0-6.

Guide to Birds of the Falkland Islands. Robin W. Woods. Anthony Nelson, Oswestry.1988. ISBN 0-904614-22-0.

Seabird and marine mammal dispersion in the waters around the Falkland Islands 1998-1999. R. W. White, J.B. Reid, A.D. Black and K.W. Gillon. Joint Nature Conservation Committee, Peterborough. 1999. ISBN 1-86107-504-9 .

Vulnerable concentrations of seabirds in Falkland Islands waters. R. W. White, K.W. Gillon, A.D. Black and J.B. Reid. Joint Nature Conservation Committee, Peterborough. 2001. ISBN 1-86107-521-9.

Wild Flowers of the Falkland Islands. Tom H. Davies & Jim H. McAdam. Bluntisham Books, Huntingdon. 1989. ISBN 1-871999-00-6.

WAR 1982

74 Days: an Islander's Diary of the Falklands Occupation 1982. John Smith. Century, London. 1984. ISBN 0-712603-61-1.

Task Force: The Falklands War, 1982. Martin Middlebrook. Penguin Books, New York. 1988. ISBN 0-14-008035-X.

The Secret War for the Falkland Islands. Nigel West. Little, Brown, London. 1997. ISBN 0-316-88226-7.

USEFUL ADDRESSES

Falklands Conservation
Falkland Islands Office: Jetty Centre, PO Box 26, Stanley, Falkland Islands
Tel: +500 22247 Fax: +500 22288
Email: conservation@horizon.co.fk
UK Office: 1 Princes Avenue, Finchley, London N3 2DA.
Tel/Fax: +44 020 8343 0831
Email: ann@falklands-nature.demon.co.uk
Website: www.falklandsconservation.com

Falkland Islands Tourist Board
John Fowler, Shackleton House, Stanley, Falkland Islands
Tel: +500 22215 Fax: +500 22619
Email: manager@tourism.org.fk
Website: www.tourism.org.fk

Travel and Holiday Arrangements
Falkland Islands Government Office,
Falkland House, 14 Broadway, London SW1 OBH
Tel: +44 020 7222 2542 Fax: +44 020 7222 2375
Email: rep@figo.u-net.com
Website: www.falklands.gov.fk
Government portal: www.falklandislands.com

Discovery Falklands (Tour Guide)
Mr Tony Smith
10 Fieldhouse Close, Stanley, Falkland Islands
Tel: +500 21027
Email: discovery@horizon.co.fk
Website: http://discoveryfalklands.freeservers.com

International Tours and Travel Ltd. (Travel Agents)
PO Box 408, Stanley, Falkland Islands
Tel: +500 22041 Fax: +500 22042
Email: int.travel@horizon.co.fk

Falkland Islands Company (Shipping Agents)
Sheena Ross, Agency Manager
Crozier Place, Stanley
Tel: +500 27630/1/2 Fax: +500 27603
Email: fic.agency@horizon.co.fk

Sulivan Shipping Services Ltd. (Shipping Agents)
Tel: +500 22626 Fax: +500 22625
Email: sulivan@horizon.co.fk

STANLEY SERVICES LIMITED
PO Box 117, Stanley, Falklands Islands
Email: abedford@stanley-services.co.fk
Tel: +500 22622 Fax: +500 22623

CHECKLIST OF FAUNA AND FLORA MENTIONED IN THE TEXT

Status is shown by the following notations:

E Endemic species   **C** Endemic subspecies

B Breeds in the Falkland Islands   (Black text) Non-breeding regular visitor   (Red text) Introduced species

MAMMALS

The Falkland Islands have no surviving native land mammals. The last Falkland wolf or Warrah was killed in 1876. Introduced land mammals other than sheep, cattle and horses include Patagonian foxes, rats, mice, rabbits, hares, cats and, on Staats Island, the guanaco. The following checklists are not comprehensive and are merely a guide to what you may see during a brief visit to the Islands. A fully comprehensive checklist can be found on the Falklands Conservation website: www.falklands-nature.demon.co.uk.

MARINE MAMMALS
Dolphins

Killer Whale	*Orcinus orca*	☐ --------------------------
Peale's Dolphin	*Lagenorhynchus australis*	☐ --------------------------
Commerson's Dolphin	*Cephalorhynchus commersonii*	☐ --------------------------

Seals

B	Southern Sea Lion	*Otaria flavescens*	☐ --------------------------
B	South American Fur Seal	*Arctocephalus australis*	☐ --------------------------
B	Southern Elephant Seal	*Mirounga leonina*	☐ --------------------------

TERRESTRIAL MAMMALS

B	Domestic/Feral Cat	*Felis catus*	☐ --------------------------
B	Norway Rat	*Rattus norvegicus*	☐ --------------------------
B	House Mouse	*Mus musculus*	☐ --------------------------
B	Patagonian Fox	*Dusicyon griseus*	☐ --------------------------
B	European Rabbit	*Oryctolagus cuniculus*	☐ --------------------------
B	Brown Hare	*Lepus capensis*	☐ --------------------------
B	Guanaco	*Lama guanicoe*	☐ --------------------------

BIRDS

e B	White-tufted Grebe	*Rollandia rolland rolland*	☐ ---------
B	Silvery Grebe	*Podiceps occipitalis occipitalis*	☐ ---------
B	Black-browed Albatross	*Diomedea melanophris*	☐ ---------
	Grey-headed Albatross	*Diomedea chrysostoma*	☐ ---------
B	Southern Giant-petrel	*Macronectes giganteus*	☐ ---------
B	Thin-billed Prion	*Pachyptila belcheri*	☐ ---------
B	Sooty Shearwater	*Puffinus griseus*	☐ ---------
B	King Penguin	*Aptenodytes patagonicus*	☐ ---------
B	Gentoo Penguin	*Pygoscelis papua papua*	☐ ---------
B	Rockhopper Penguin	*Eudyptes chrysocome chrysocome*	☐ ---------
B	Magellanic Penguin	*Spheniscus magellanicus*	☐ ---------
B	Rock Cormorant	*Phalacrocorax magellanicus*	☐ ---------
B	King Cormorant	*Phalacrocorax atriceps albiventer*	☐ ---------
e B	Black-crowned Night heron	*Nycticorax nycticorax falklandicus*	☐ ---------
B	Black-necked Swan	*Cygnus melancoryphus*	☐ ---------
B	Ruddy-headed Goose	*Chloephaga rubidiceps*	☐ ---------
e B	Upland Goose	*Chloephaga picta leucoptera*	☐ ---------
e B	Kelp Goose	*Chloephaga hybrida malvinarum*	☐ ---------
B	Patagonian Crested-duck	*Anas specularioides specularioides*	☐ ---------
E B	Falkland Flightless Steamer-duck	*Tachyeres brachypterus*	☐ ---------
B	Flying Steamer-duck	*Tachyeres patachonicus*	☐ ---------
B	Speckled Teal	*Anas flavirostris*	☐ ---------
B	Chiloë Wigeon	*Anas sibilatrix*	☐ ---------
B	Silver Teal	*Anas versicolor fretensis*	☐ ---------
B	Turkey Vulture	*Cathartes aura falklandicus*	☐ ---------
B	Red-backed Hawk	*Buteo polyosoma polyosoma*	☐ ---------
B	Striated Caracara	*Phalcoboenus australis*	☐ ---------
B	Crested Caracara	*Caracara plancus plancus*	☐ ---------
B	Peregrine Falcon	*Falco peregrinus cassini*	☐ ---------
	White-winged Coot	*Fulica leucoptera*	☐ ---------
B	Two-banded Plover	*Charadrius falklandicus*	☐ ---------
B	Rufous-chested Dotterel	*Charadrius modestus*	☐ ---------

B	Blackish Oystercatcher	*Haematopus ater*	☐ --------------------------
B	Magellanic Oystercatcher	*Haematopus leucopodus*	☐ --------------------------
B	Magellanic Snipe	*Gallinago magellanica*	☐ --------------------------
	White-rumped Sandpiper	*Calidris fuscicollis*	☐ --------------------------
	Snowy Sheathbill	*Chionis alba*	☐ --------------------------
B	Falkland Skua	*Catharacta antarctica*	☐ --------------------------
B	Dolphin Gull	*Larus scoresbii*	☐ --------------------------
B	Kelp Gull	*Larus dominicanus*	☐ --------------------------
B	Brown-hooded Gull	*Larus maculipennis*	☐ --------------------------
B	South American Tern	*Sterna hirundinacea*	☐ --------------------------
e B	Short-eared Owl	*Asio flammeus sanfordi*	☐ --------------------------
e B	Tussac-bird	*Cinclodes antarcticus antarcticus*	☐ --------------------------
e B	Dark-faced Ground-tyrant	*Muscisaxicola macloviana*	☐ --------------------------
e B	Grass Wren	*Cistothorus platensis falklandicus*	☐ --------------------------
E B	Cobb's Wren	*Troglodytes cobbi*	☐ --------------------------
e B	Falkland Thrush	*Turdus falcklandii falcklandii*	☐ --------------------------
e B	Falkland Pipit	*Anthus correndera grayi*	☐ --------------------------
e B	Black-throated Finch	*Melanodera melanodera melanodera*	☐ --------------------------
e B	Long-tailed Meadowlark	*Sturnella loyca falklandica*	☐ --------------------------
B	Black-chinned Siskin	*Carduelis barbata*	☐ --------------------------
B	House Sparrow	*Passer domesticus*	☐ --------------------------

FLORA

	Balsam-bog	*Bolax gummifera*	☐ --------------------------
	Berry-lobelia	*Pratia repens*	☐ --------------------------
	California Club-rush	*Schoenoplectus californicus*	☐ --------------------------
	Cinnamon grass	*Hierochloe redolens*	☐ --------------------------
E	Clubmoss Cudweed	*Chevreulia lycopodioides*	☐ --------------------------
E	Coastal Nassauvia	*Nassauvia gaudichaudii*	☐ --------------------------
	Curled Dock	*Rumex crispus*	☐ --------------------------
	Diddle-dee	*Empetrum rubrum*	☐ --------------------------

	Common Name	Scientific Name		
	Dog Orchid	*Codonorchis lessonii*	☐	------
	Emerald Bog	*Colobanthus subulatus*	☐	------
	European Gorse	*Ulex europaeus*	☐	------
	Fachine	*Chiliotrichum diffusum*	☐	------
E	Felton's Flower	*Calandrinia feltonii*	☐	------
	Fox and Cubs	*Hieracium aurantiacum*	☐	------
	Foxtail Barley	*Hordeum jubatum*	☐	------
	Fuegian Couch	*Elymus glaucescens*	☐	------
	Fuegian Yellow Violet	*Viola magellanica*	☐	------
	Gaudichaud's Orchid	*Chloraea gaudichaudii*	☐	------
E	Hairy Daisy	*Erigeron incertus*	☐	------
	Hooker's Sweet Cicely	*Oreomyrrhis hookeri*	☐	------
	Lady's slipper	*Calceolaria fothergillii*	☐	------
	Monterey Cypress	*Cupressus macrocarpa*	☐	------
	Native Yellow Violet	*Viola maculata*	☐	------
	New Zealand Cabbage-palm	*Cordyline australis*	☐	------
	New Zealand Flax	*Phormium tenax*	☐	------
	Pale Maiden	*Olsynium filifolium*	☐	------
	Pale Yellow Orchid	*Gavilea australis*	☐	------
	Pigvine	*Gunnera magellanica*	☐	------
	Pimpernel	*Anagallis alternifolia*	☐	------
	Scurvygrass	*Oxalis enneaphylla*	☐	------
	Sea Cabbage	*Senecio candidans*	☐	------
	Sheep's Sorrel	*Rumex acetosella*	☐	------
	Shore meadow-grass	*Poa robusta*	☐	------
E	Silvery Buttercup	*Hamadryas argentea*	☐	------
	Small Fern	*Blechnum penna-marina*	☐	------
E	Smooth Ragwort	*Senecio vaginatus*	☐	------
E	Snake Plant	*Nassauvia serpens*	☐	------
	Sundew	*Drosera uniflora*	☐	------
	Tall Fern	*Blechnum magellanicum*	☐	------
	Tall Rush	*Marsippospermum grandiflorum*	☐	------
	Teaberry	*Myrteola nummularia*	☐	------

Tussac	*Poa flabellata*	☐ -
ⓔ Vanilla Daisy	*Leucheria suaveolens*	☐ -
Whitegrass	*Cortaderia pilosa*	☐ -
Whitlowgrass	*Draba funiculosa*	☐ -
Wild Celery	*Apium australe*	☐ -
ⓔ Woolly Ragwort	*Senecio littoralis*	☐ -
Yellow Orchid	*Gavilea littoralis*	☐ -
Yellow Pale Maiden	*Sisyrinchium chilense*	☐ -

☐ -
☐ -
☐ -
☐ -
☐ -
☐ -
☐ -
☐ -
☐ -
☐ -
☐ -
☐ -
☐ -
☐ -
☐ -
☐ -
☐ -
☐ -

PHOTOGRAPHIC CREDITS

Page 3. Lars Eric Lindblad and Roddy Napier; West Point Garden; Peter Clement; 1994.

Page 4. Debbie Summers; Author; Johnsons Harbour; Becky Ingham; 2001.

Page 5. Becky Ingham; Conservation Officer; Stanley; Debbie Summers; 2001.

Page 6. John A T Fowler; Tourist Board Manager; Miami; Atsuko Livoti-Mogi; 1998/99.

Page 9. Sven-Olof Lindblad.

Page 10. Road cutting through stone run; East Falklands; Peter J Pepper.

Page 12. Black-browed albatross; At sea off Argentina; Andy Swash/WildGuides.
Elephant seal; male; Sea Lion Island; Richard W White/JNCC; 1998.
King penguin; Volunteer Point; Richard W White/JNCC; 2000.
Yellow orchid; Carcass Island; Nick Woods; 1996.

Page 13. Cruise Visitors; Leopard Beach, Carcass Island, West Falklands; Debbie Summers; 2000.

Page 14. King penguins; Falklands Conservation.

Page 15. Allan White.

Page 16. Rockhopper penguin; Kevin Schafer.

Page 17. Photographer with penguins; Kidney Island; Richard W White/JNCC; 1998.

Page 19. Stanley harbour; 19th Century; Schulz/FI Museum & National Trust Collection; c. 1890.

Page 20. 3 Riders just off for beef; Goddard/FI Museum & National Trust Collection.

Page 21. Notice to mariners; Chart; Stanley Harbour & Port William; FI Museum & National Trust Collection; 1867.

Page 22. Sheep shearing; Billy Poole; J. Leonard.

Page 23. Wedding party; Somewhere in Camp; Ferguson Collection.
Mrs Macaskill; Pat Luxton.
Frank Smith with the Nancy in the background; Central Office, Property of FIG; c. 1980's.
Shearing gang; Somewhere in Camp; Goddard/FI Museum & National Trust Collection; 1896.

Page 24. View of Port Louis-Berkeley Sound; East Falklands; Mrs Chorley Collection/Dean Family; 1838-39.

Page 25. Cape Pembroke lighthouse; East Falklands; Keith Gillon; 2000.
Squid jigging vessel; Kevin Schafer; 2000.

Page 26. Brown-hooded Gull; summer plumage; Kevin Schafer.
Brown-hooded Gull; winter plumage; Andy Black/JNCC; 1999.
Entering Stanley harbour; undated.

Page 27. The hulks of the *Egeria* and the *William Shand* with the *Snowsquall* and the SS *Falkland*; Stanley; Smith Collection.
The Lady Elizabeth; FI Museum & National Trust Collection.
Hulk of the *Jhelum*; Stanley Harbour; John Carr Images.

Page 28. Stanley twinning sign; Outside the town of Stanley; John Carr Images.
Stanley waterfront; c.1915.

Page 29. Governor Richard Clement Moody; Governor of the Fi between 1842-1848; Falkland Island Archives.
Stanley waterfront; undated.

Page 30. Southern giant petrel; Falkland Islands; Gordon Langsbury.
Kelp gull; Richard W White/JNCC; 2000.
Black-crowned night heron; Carcass Island; Kevin Schafer; 2000.
Jubilee Villas; Kevin Schafer; 2000.

Page 31. Stanley from the air; Falklands Conservation.
Signpost; Kevin Schafer; 2000.

Page 32. 1982 War Memorial; John Carr Images.
Government House; John Carr Images.
Christ Church Cathedral and Whalebone Arch; John Carr Images.

Page 33. Typical Falkland house; Stanley; Nigel Hawks.
View of Fitzroy Road, Stanley; Stanley; John Carr Images.

Aerial View of Port William, Cape Pembroke and Stanley; BAS/Dept of Agricuture; 1999.

Page 34. Britten Norman Islander; Falklands Conservation.

Page 35. Aerial view of Sea Lion island; RAF Mount Pleasant 16/3/98 No 1312/MRR/042/31.

Page 36. Black-necked swans; Seabirds at Sea/JNCC.
Arthur Cobb; 3rd from left; Bleaker Island; Cobb Collection; 1911.

Page 38. Dog orchid; Carcass Island; Nick Woods; November 1999.
Ruddy-headed goose; Kevin Schafer; 2000.

Page 39. Long Gulch; Bleaker Island; Mike Rendell.
Yellow orchid; Carcass Island; Nick Woods; 1996.

Page 40. Commerson's Dolphins; Kevin Schafer.
South American tern; D Gray.

Page 41. Leopard beach; Carcass Island; Kevin Schafer; 2000.

Page 43. The settlement and its gardens; Carcass Island; Kevin Schafer; 2000.
Sea cabbage; Saunders Island; Kevin Schafer; 2000.

Page 44. Black-chinned siskin; Carcass Island; Kevin Schafer; 2000.
Black-throated finch; Sea Lion Island; Kevin Schafer; 2000.
Magellanic penguin; Kevin Schafer; 2000.

Page 45. Berry-lobelia; Nick Woods; 1996.
Rob McGill; Kevin Schafer; 2000.
The view across Port Pattison; Carcass Island; Kevin Schafer; 2000.

Page 46. Elephant seal; male; D Gray.
Cobb's wren; Sea Lion Island; Kevin Schafer; 2000

Page 47. Gentoo penguins; Kevin Schafer; 2000

Page 48. Vickers Gun; Gypsy Cove; Kevin Schafer; 2000
Woolly ragwort; Kidney Island; Nick Woods; November 1996.

Page 49. Peregrine; Falkland Islands; Gordon Langsbury.

Page 50. Magellanic oystercatcher; Kevin Schafer.
Blackish oystercatcher; Seabirds at Sea/JNCC.

Page 51. Gypsy Cove from the south; Kevin Schafer.

Page 52. Falkland skua; Volunteer Point, E Falklands; Richard W White/JNCC; 1999.

Upland goose; Kevin Schafer.

Page 53. Turkey vulture; Kevin Schafer;

Page 54. King penguin; Richard W White/JNCC.

Magellanic penguin; Kevin Schafer.

Gentoo penguin; Antarctica; Andy Swash/Wildguides.

Rockhopper penguin; Richard W White/JNCC.

Rockhopper penguin colony; Kidney Cove; Kevin Schafer.

Page 55. Kidney Island from Mount Low; Kevin Schafer.

Page 56. Sooty shearwater; photographer unknown.

Page 57. Red-backed hawk; Nigel Hawks.

Page 58. Native yellow violet; Carcass Island; Nick Woods.

Page 60. Crested caracara; Seabirds at Sea/JNCC.

Striated caracara; Kevin Schafer.

Page 61. The North End; New Island; Kevin Schafer.

Page 62. Black-browed albatross; adult and chick; Kevin Schafer.

Page 63. Gentoo penguin; North End colony; Kevin Schafer.

Gentoo penguin; coming ashore; Kevin Schafer.

Page 64. Western coast; New Island South; Ian J Strange.

Rockhopper penguin; Settlement colony; New Island South; Ian J Strange.

Page 66. Scurvygrass; Ian J Strange.

Settlement; New Island; Ian J Strange.

Looking towards Beaver Island; Ian J Strange.

South American fur seals; basking on rocks; Ian J Strange.

Page 67. Beef and Coffin Islands; Ian J Strange.

Magellanic Snipe; Kevin Schafer.

Page 68. Snake plant; Long Island Mountain; Nick Woods; December 1999.

Sheep shearing; Nigel Hawks.

Page 69. Port Howard settlement; Nigel Hawks.

Page 70. Tourist with rockhopper penguins; Kevin Schafer.

Page 71. Black-browed albatross; Chick being weighed; Falklands Conservation/Nic Huin; 1999.

Black-browed albatross; clifftop colony; Nigel Hawks.

Page 72. Rainbow and outhouse; Kevin Schafer; 2000.

Silvery grebe; Kevin Schafer; 2000.

White-tufted grebe; Falkland Islands; Gordon Langsbury.

Page 73. The view across the Neck; Saunders Island; Allan White.

Page 74. Trypot; FI Museum & National Trust Collection.

Rockhopper penguin claw marks; Kevin Schafer.

Page 75. Lady's slipper; Nigel Hawks.

Silvery buttercup; Bertha's Beach; David Broughton; October 1999.

Pale maiden; Kidney Island; Nick Woods; November 1999.

Hairy daisy; Carcass Island; Nick Woods November 1999.

Page 76. Peale's dolphin; Todd Pusser.

Rufous-chested dotterel; Sea Lion Island; Keith Gillon; 1998.

Page 77. Elephant seal; male; Sea Lion Island; Richard W White/JNCC; 1998.

Elephant seals; basking; Kevin Schafer; 2000.

Page 78. Southern sea lion; male; Beauchêne Island; Richard W White/JNCC; 2000.

Tussacbird; Kevin Schafer; 2000.

Page 79. Tussac grass; Sea Lion Island; Kevin Schafer; 2000.

Page 80. Rockhopper Point; Sea Lion Island; Kevin Schafer; 2000.

Killer whale; Shetland Islands, UK; Hugh Harrop.

Page 81. King cormorants; resting on rock platform; Kevin Schafer; 2000.

Magellanic penguins; Kevin Schafer; 2000.

Kelp; Kevin Schafer; 2000.

Page 82. Vanilla daisy; Mew Island (North); Nick Woods; November 1999.

View across the Jasons; Dr Andrea Clausen/Falklands Conservation.

Page 83. Dolphin gull; Kevin Schafer; 2000.

Page 84. Grass wren; Richard W White/JNCC.

Coasta nassauvia; New Island (North); Nick Woods; November 1999.

Page 86. Teaberry; Kidney Island; Nick Woods; 1996.

Falkland thrush; Kevin Schafer; 2000.

Page 87. Fachine; Canopus Hill, near Stanley; Nick Woods; December 1999.

Page 88. Flying steamer duck; Kevin Schafer; 2000.

Falkland flightless steamer duck; Kevin Schafer; 2000.

Page 89. Long-tailed meadowlark; Kevin Schafer; 2000.

King penguins; Volunteer Point; Kevin Schafer; 2000.

Page 90. King cormorant; D Gray.

Rock cormorant; Gordon Langsbury.

Page 91. Sandy beach; Volunteer Point; Richard W White/JNCC; 1999.

Page 92. The Weddell Inn; Nigel Hawks.

Patagonian crested duck; Seabirds at Sea/JNCC.

Page 93. Tidal creek; Weddell Island; Nigel Hawks.

Dark-faced ground-tyrant; Seabirds at Sea/JNCC.

Whitlowgrass; New Island (North); Nick Woods; November 1999.

Falkland pipit; Kevin Schafer; 2000.

Page 94. Striated caracara; investigating camera gear; Falklands Conservation.

The new landing ramp; West Point Island; Roddy Napier.

Page 95. Lily and Roddy Napier; Allan White.

Page 96. Arthur Felton; undated.

Felton's flower; West Point Island; Nick Woods; December 1996.

Page 97; The Settlement; West Point Island; Kevin Schafer; 2000.

Clubmoss cudweed; Carcass Island; Nick Woods; November 1999.

Hooker's sweet cicely; Carcass Island; Nick Woods; November 1999.

Two-banded plover; Kevin Schafer; 2000.

Black-browed albatross; nestling; Kevin Schafer; 2000.

Page 98. Rockhopper penguins; walking through tussac; Kevin Schafer; 2000.

FALKLANDS CONSERVATION

The Charity that Takes Action for Nature in the Falkland Islands

Patron: HRH The Duke of York

HOW YOU CAN HELP US

Your support is vital to enable us to continue our work. Please complete the form below to indicate how you wish to help: by becoming a member, making a donation, through a pledge in your will, or supporting a current conservation project.

Your Name _____

Your Address _____

_____

_____ Post Code _____

Indicate by ticking box as appropriate:

☐ **I wish to become a Member of Falklands Conservation and receive regular updates on Falklands wildlife and conservation work in the Islands.**
ANNUAL SUBSCRIPTION RATES:
FI/UK only: Ordinary £15, Benefactor £50, Life £500
Overseas: Ordinary £20/$40, Benefactor £55/$110, Life £600/$1,000

☐ **I wish to make a special contribution to a current conservation project.**

☐ **Please send me further details.I wish to make a donation to support the work of Falklands Conservation.**
Your contribution, large or small, will make a real difference.

☐ **I wish to leave a legacy to Falklands Conservation in my will. Please send me a pledge form and further details.**
A bequest in your will is a vital way of helping to protect Falklands wildlife for future generations.

I ENCLOSE:
Membership Subscription ☐

Donation ☐

TOTAL* ☐
*Please make cheques payable to Falklands Conservation , or
*I wish to pay by Access/Visa.

I authorise you to debit my Access/Visa account with the amount

£ _____

My Access/Visa number is:

☐☐☐☐ ☐☐☐☐ ☐☐☐☐ ☐☐☐☐

☐☐☐☐ Signature _____
Expiry date

Cardholder s Name _____

Cardholder s Address *(if different from applicant)* _____

_____

_____ Post Code _____